GRAPHIC DESIGN
WORKBOOK

professional standard
design school ✦✦✦✦

FIRST PRINTING

Feb. 2019

All rights reserved.

No part of this book may be reproduced or transmitted in any form or by any means (electronic, photocopying, recording or otherwise) without written permission of the copyright holder. Please note that all of the materials that you receive from Chaya Murik are copyrighted and may not be shared without written permission. If a student would like to reproduce lecture presentations, course notes or other similar materials provided by instructors, he/she must obtain the written consent from Professional Standard Design School / Chaya Murik beforehand. Class notes may not be shared or distributed in any form. Otherwise all such reproduction is an infringement of copyright and is absolutely prohibited.

Copyright © 2019
Chaya Murik
1204 Medina Road
Lakewood, NJ 08701
graphics@chayamurik.com

ISBN: 9781795810661

ABOUT THIS WORKBOOK

"Keep away from people who try to belittle your ambitions. Small people always do that, but the really great make you feel that you, too, can become great."

— Mark Twain

This workbook is to be used in cunjuction with the Professional Standard Design School Course.

THE GRAPHIC DESIGN COURSE AT PROFESSIONAL STANDARD DESIGN SCHOOL is a project-based graphics design class that uses common designer projects to teach techniques in Adobe Illustrator, InDesign, and Photoshop. With hands-off guidance, students learn to research, plan, and execute their design using all the tools available to graphic artists both online and off. There is particular emphasis on brainstorming, research, and marketing. This learning experience enables students to become independent graphic designers with a clear understanding of marketing through print media. At the end of this project-based course, the student will have achieved basic proficiency in the Adobe programs together with a clear grasp of the design principles and four portfolio pieces of work.

ABOUT THE AUTHOR
Hi, my name is Chaya Murik and I started my career by publishing a coloring book when I was ten years old. We all start somewhere, right? Since then I have focused on building my career by studying design and marketing at the Manchester College of Arts and Technology and even achieved one of the top 5 marks in the UK. I recently finished my MBA with a Marketing concentration. I then went on to convince the staff at Oorah to give me a shot and I quickly rose to become a Senior Graphic Designer in their marketing department.

Nowadays I love to teach all aspects of graphic design. Coaching my students and making them the best designers they can be is my passion and many of them leave my courses and go on to create full designing careers of their own. In addition to learning, teaching and eating copious amounts of watermelon and raspberry Jelly Bellies, I also design magazines, logos and other print media from my home studio.

UNIT ONE
THE BASICS

There is no formula for
creativity-
but there's definitely a flowing form in
the way highly creative people glide
toward exciting endless ideas...

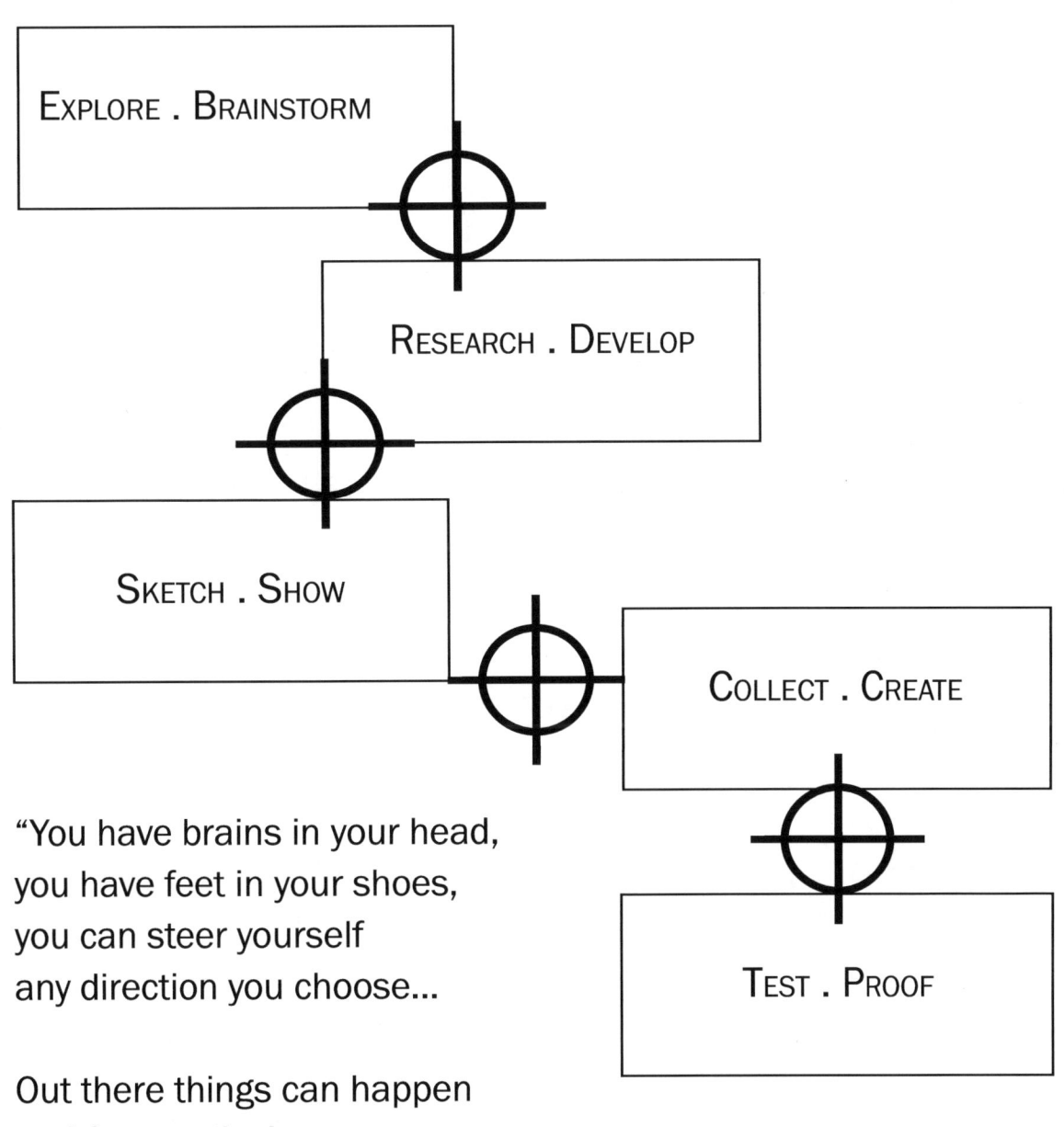

"You have brains in your head,
you have feet in your shoes,
you can steer yourself
any direction you choose...

Out there things can happen
and frequently do
to people as brainy
and footsy as you"

--Dr. Seuss
Oh, the Places You'll Go

THE MARKETING MIX

Product

Promotion

Place

Price

⊕ WHAT IS GRAPHIC DESIGN?

⊕ HOW DID IT EVOLVE?

⊕ WHEN DID THE PROFESSION COME INTO EXISTENCE?

⊕ AND WHY?

What is the information that needs to be passed on? When the audience reads your book/ webpage/ ad what's he supposed to get out of it?

When a graphic designer gets a job, be it a poster design, book design, web design, advertising, he has to start with asking himself the following fundamental questions:

- What is the objective of the communication
- What needs to be said first and then next and then after that? (levels of hierarchy)
- How do you want the eye to flow through the page?
- What is the tone of voice?
- Who are you speaking to?

• The term graphic design can refer to a number of artistic and professional disciplines which focus on visual communication and presentation.

• Various methods are used to create and combine symbols, images and/or words to create a visual representation of ideas and messages.

• When people need to necessarily express something, usually with an aim towards promotion or information dispensing, the focus becomes how best to do it.

• Graphic design was born of art and technology (printing).

WHICH PROGRAM SHOULD I USE?

Adobe InDesign, Photoshop and Illustrator are part of the Adobe Creative Cloud of applications. They contain "breakthrough interactive design tools that enable you to create, deliver, and optimize beautiful, high-impact digital experiences across media and devices." InDesign, Photoshop and Illustrator are some of the best-known applications included in the Adobe CC and are the industry standard tools for graphic design. InDesign, Photoshop and Illustrator each perform specific functions in design and designers use them with one another.

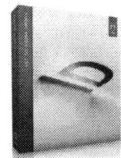

ADOBE INDESIGN

Design and lay out documents with InDesign. An essential tool in print production, InDesign offers control over typography and page placement to create books, magazines, newspapers and catalogs. Graphic designers import Photoshop and Illustrator files into InDesign to create finished pieces and prepare them for publication.

INDESIGN IS GENERALLY USED FOR:
- Editorial design
- Book design
- Multiple page brochures
- Print campaigns
- Stationary systems
- Annual reports
- Interactive PDF documents

ADOBE PHOTOSHOP

Edit images with Photoshop. This advanced image editing program contains countless features for creating, manipulating and perfecting images. Photoshop is essential to professional photographers, who use for everything from removing stray hairs to changing the background of an image. Graphic designers use it to draw and paint original images or combine and manipulate existing images.

PHOTOSHOP IS GENERALLY USED FOR:
- Photo enhancement
- Photo color correction
- Photo manipulation
- Software/Web/Mobile apps design
- Web graphics
- Motion graphics
- Special effects

ADOBE ILLUSTRATOR

Create graphic illustrations that go from the size of a postage stamp to the size of sports arena sign with Illustrator. The vector format that Illustrator produces are "resolution independent," so their size is easy to change. Most images have a fixed resolution, meaning that if you expand them to a larger size than the resolution allows, the image will distort.

ILLUSTRATOR IS GENERALLY USED FOR:
- Logo
- Logotype
- Monograms
- Vector painting
- Illustrations
- Type setting for stationary systems
- Print campaigns
- Web graphics

Never use Photoshop to create logo's. The obvious reason is because pixel data cannot be enlarged without distortion. If you create the logo in vector format, your logo will be scalable to any size forever.

KEYWORDS & CONCEPTS

BASICS FOR PRINT DESIGN:

PIXEL (PICTURE ELEMENT) _____

300 DPI 72 DPI _____

VECTOR GRAPHICS _____

LINKS _____

COLOR MODES: CMYK RGB _____

SPOT COLOR _____

GRAYSCALE _____

PMS (PANTONE MATCHING SYSTEM) _____

SWATCHES _____

BLEED _____

CROP MARKS _____

SLUG _____

GUTTER _____

MARGINS _____

SAFE AREA _____

BASICS WHEN CREATING:

VIEW MODES _____

LAYERS _____

GUIDES _____

SELECTION AND DIRECT SELECTION TOOLS _____

SCALING: _____

STROKE AND FILL_____

SHADOW_____

FEATHER_____

NAVIGATION TOOLS_____

ZOOM AND HAND TOOLS_____

BOUNDING BOX_____

MODIFYING KEYS: SHIFT ALT AND CONTROL_____

KEYBOARD SHORT CUTS_____

COPY_____

PASTE_____

UNDO_____

SELECT ALL_____

FIT IN WINDOW_____

BASICS FOR TYPE:

TYPE TOOLS : AREA TYPE AND TYPE ON PATH TOOLS_____

INSTALLING FONTS_____

BODY_____

KERNING_____

LEADING_____

LIGATURE_____

POINT_____

ROMAN TYPE_____

ALLEY_____

SERIF_____

SANS SERIF TYPEFACE_____

TOMBSTONING_____

ORPHAN_____

WIDOW_____

RESOLUTION & DPI

WHAT IS D.P.I. AND HOW IT WILL AFFECT YOUR PRINTED JOB?
D.P.I. or "Dots per Inch" is the measurement used within the printing and graphics design industry to determine how sharp an image is.
WEB GRAPHICS and online photos are normally created at 72dpi (dots per inch). This low resolution is great for the web because the images look excellent on a computer monitor and the file sizes are very small which helps web pages load faster. However, when designing graphics for commercial PRINTING purposes, your images should be 300dpi or better.

Checking the Resolution of an Image in Photoshop:

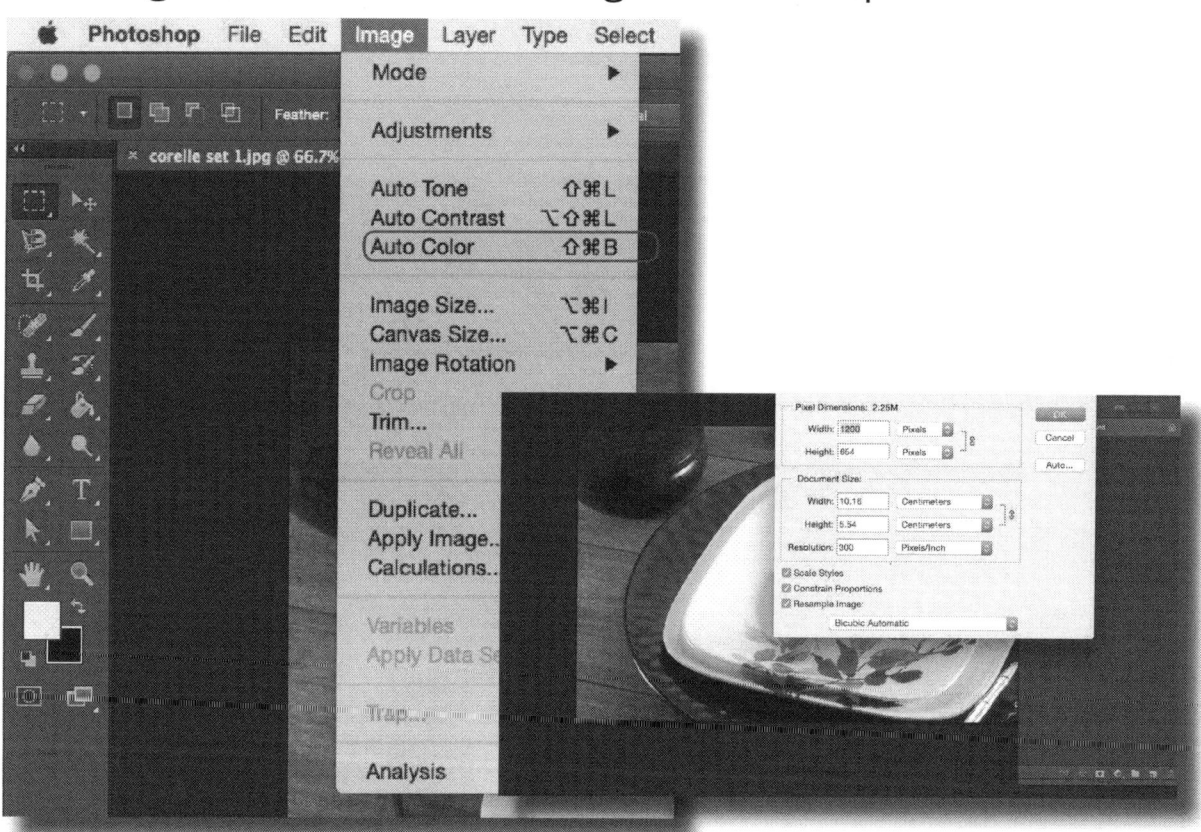

RESAMPLING AND INTERPOLATION - WHY RESIZING ISN'T THE ANSWER
All artwork design programs allow you to resize an image you are working on, but it's important to understand why simply resizing a low resolution image will not produce a true high resolution image. When you resize and make a low resolution image larger to meet the commercial printing specifications of 300DPI, all you are really doing is stretching the image. The technical term is called either resampling or interpolation. Since high resolution images are based upon the number of pixels an image contains, resizing will not create new pixels, information of your images and will only make each pixel larger by stretching it. The only way to ensure picture perfect high quality printing of your photos and images is to start with a high resolution image obtainable by the methods mentioned above.

PRACTICE PROJECT

"Practice is the best of all instructors"

— Publilius Syrus

Project: A booklet describing the 10 plagues, each page with a description of the plague and a manipulated photo. Must Include front and back Cover.

✢ Start by writing down ideas for colors and layouts. (Refer back to the design process sheet to see structure of how to begin with layout, brainstorm, research...).

✢ Decide on measurements and sizes for your book.

✢ Sketch ideas and concepts on paper.

✢ Draft on the computer.

✢ Test/Show the layout.

✢ Design one spread, then you will create master pages to have the design consistent through the book.

✢ As you follow through each plague manipulate the images Photoshop as needed.

✢ Remember to keep sketching as you come up with ideas/concepts so you can monitor your train of thought and keep any ideas for later use.

✢ Evaluate you work with an essay explaining your design process and the way in which you came to your end product.

Components:
(provided digitally)

Raw Photos

Text for each of
The Ten Plagues.

Good luck.

INSPIRATION

Every designers' dirty little secret is that they copy other designers' work. They see work they like, and they imitate it. Rather cheekily, they call this inspiration.

— Aaron Russell

Design is an opportunity to continue telling the story, not just to sum everything up.

— Tate Linden

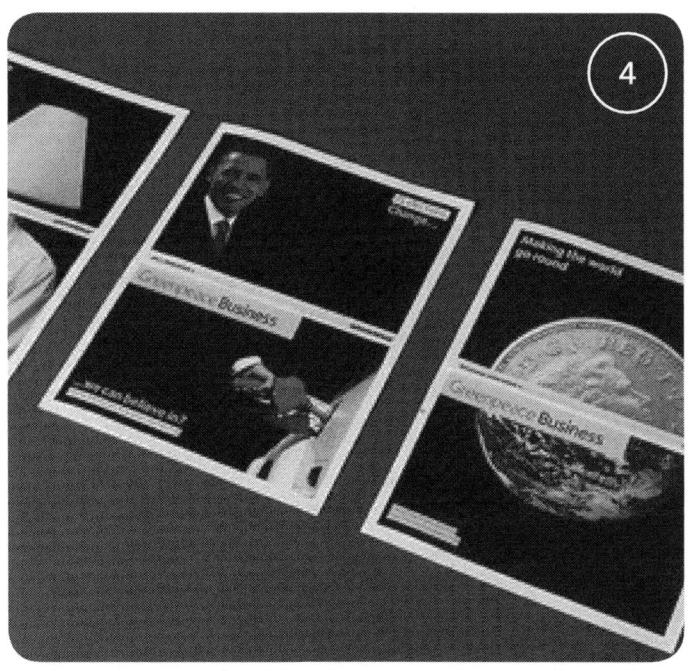

INDESIGN TOOLBOX

The toolbox contains the main tools for designing. Click any tool to select and use it.

A small arrow next to a tool in the toolbox indicates that the tool also has additional options available. In Photoshop, click and hold your mouse on a tool to see its options. For example, if you click and hold on the select tool, you'll see select options such as eliptical selction, single row selection, etc.

Tool Options
When you select a tool, additional options appear in the Tool Options bar (by default this is located just below the main menu).

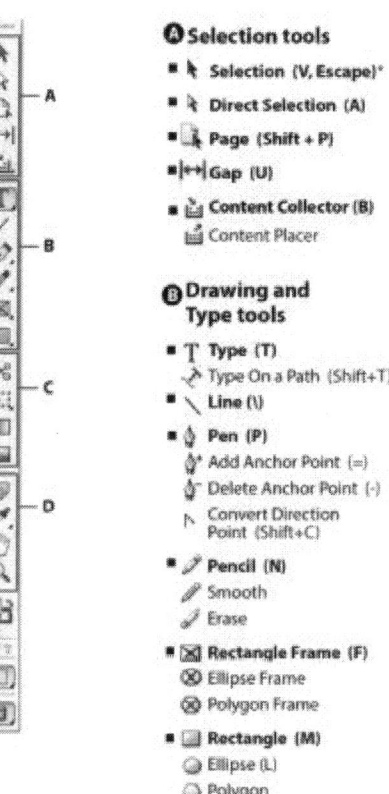

Toolbox overview

A Selection tools
- Selection (V, Escape)*
- Direct Selection (A)
- Page (Shift + P)
- Gap (U)
- Content Collector (B)
  - Content Placer

B Drawing and Type tools
- Type (T)
  - Type On a Path (Shift+T)
- Line (\)
- Pen (P)
  - Add Anchor Point (=)
  - Delete Anchor Point (-)
  - Convert Direction Point (Shift+C)
- Pencil (N)
  - Smooth
  - Erase
- Rectangle Frame (F)
  - Ellipse Frame
  - Polygon Frame
- Rectangle (M)
  - Ellipse (L)
  - Polygon

C Transformation tools
- Scissors (C)
- Free Transform (E)
  - Rotate (R)
  - Scale (S)
  - Shear (O)
- Gradient Swatch (G)
- Gradient Feather (Shift+G)

D Modification and Navigation tools
- Note
- Eyedropper (I)
  - Measure (K)
- Hand (H)
- Zoom (Z)

"We can't solve problems by using the same kind of thinking we used when we created them."

— Albert Einstein

selection tools
INDESIGN TOOLBOX

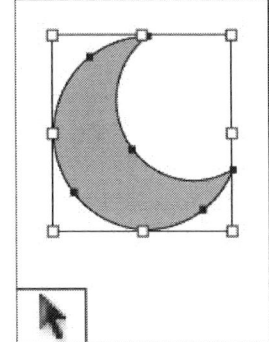

Tool: _____

Function: _____

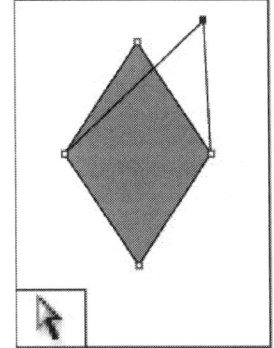

Tool: _____

Function: _____

Tool: _____

Function: _____

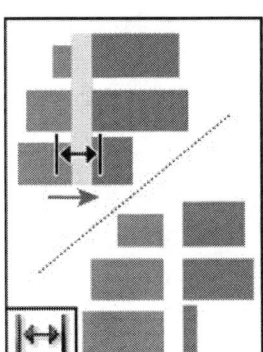

Tool: _____

Function: _____

Design is not the narrow application of formal skills, it is a way of thinking.

— Chris Pullman

drawing & type tools
INDESIGN TOOLBOX

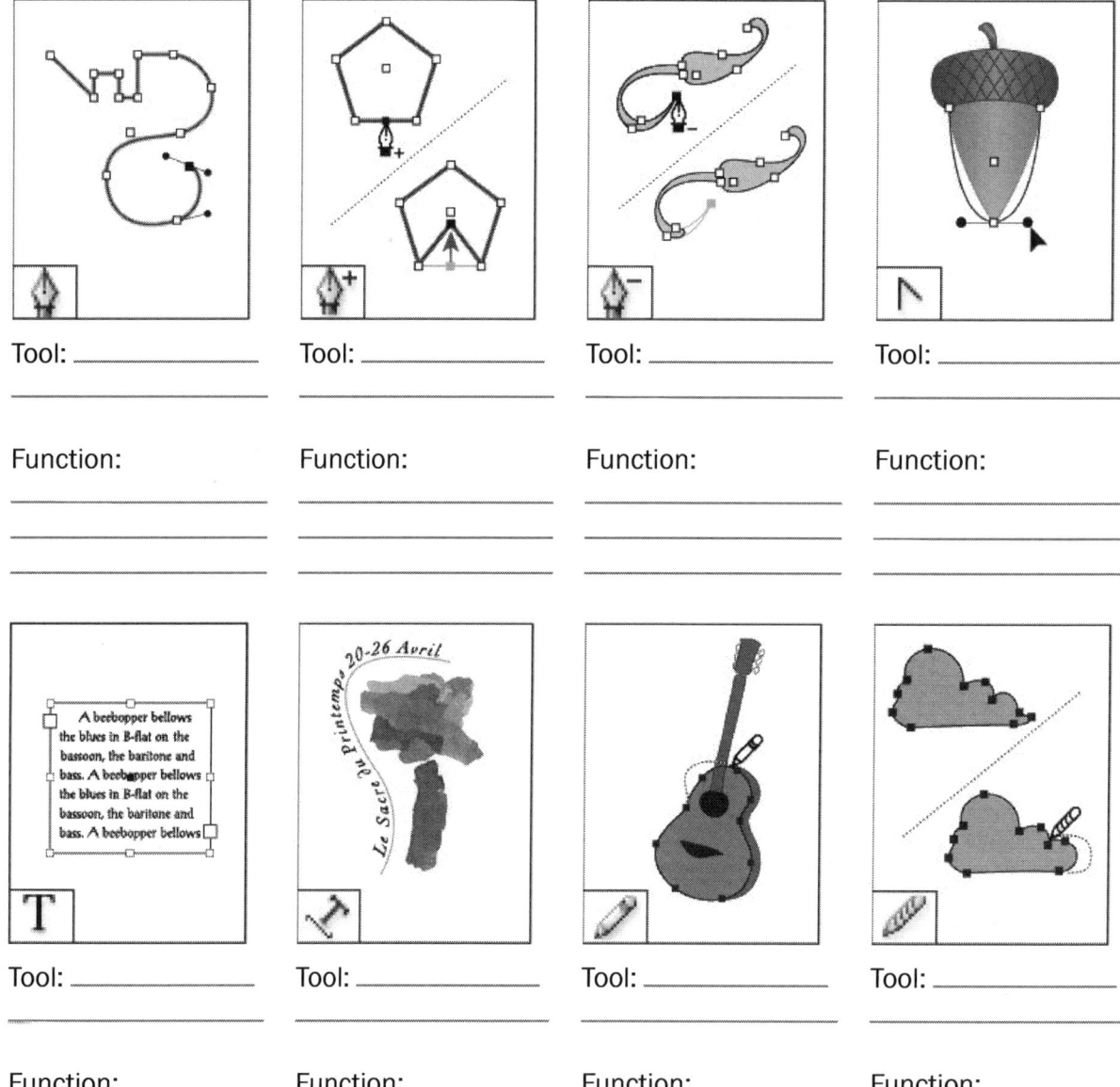

Tool: _____

Function:

Tool: _____

Function:

Tool: _____

Function:

Tool: _____

Function:

Tool: _____

Function:

Tool: _____

Function:

Tool: _____

Function:

Tool: _____

Function:

> You can't do better design with a computer,
> but you can speed up your work enormously.
>
> — Wim Crouwel

drawing & type tools

INDESIGN TOOLBOX

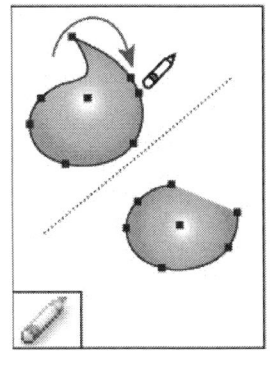

Tool: _____

Function: _____

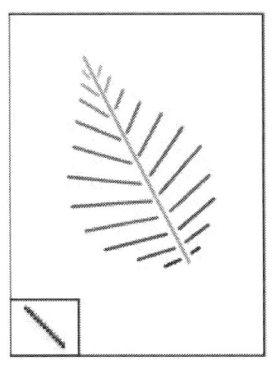

Tool: _____

Function: _____

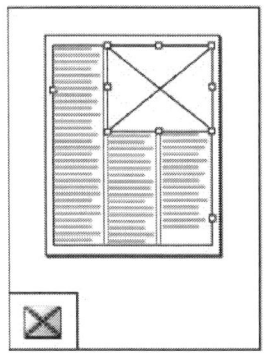

Tool: _____

Function: _____

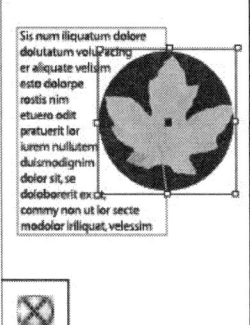

Tool: _____

Function: _____

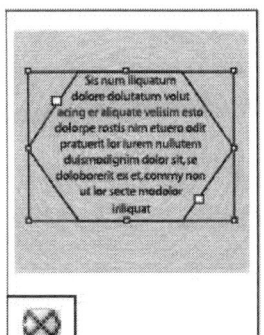

Tool: _____

Function: _____

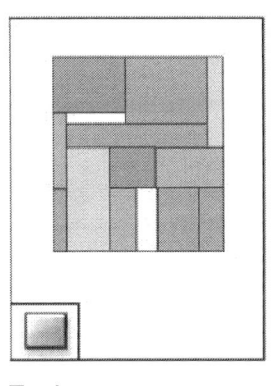

Tool: _____

Function: _____

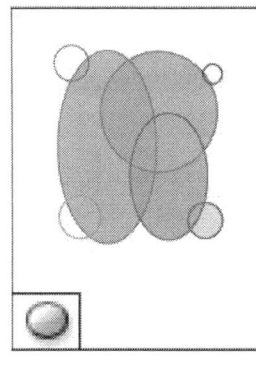

Tool: _____

Function: _____

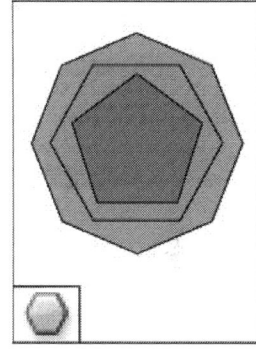

Tool: _____

Function: _____

> Computers are to design as microwaves are to cooking.
>
> — Milton Glaser

transformation tools
INDESIGN TOOLBOX

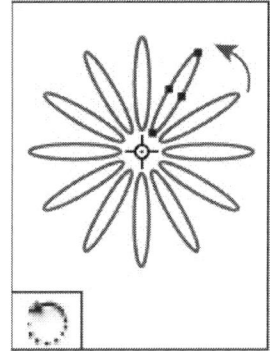

Tool: _____

Function: _____
_____

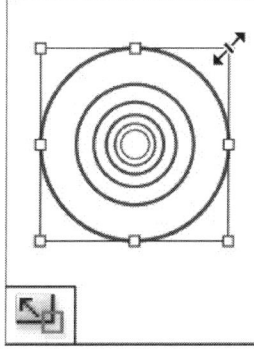

Tool: _____

Function: _____
_____

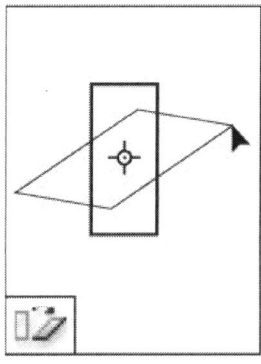

Tool: _____

Function: _____
_____

Tool: _____

Function: _____
_____

modification & navigation tools

INDESIGN TOOLBOX

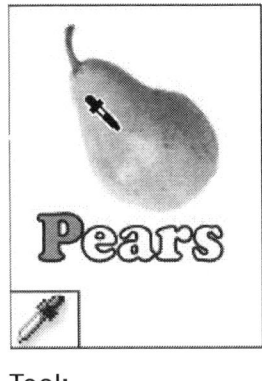

Tool: _____

Function: _____

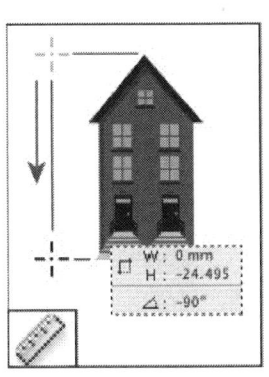

Tool: _____

Function: _____

Tool: _____

Function: _____

Tool: _____

Function: _____

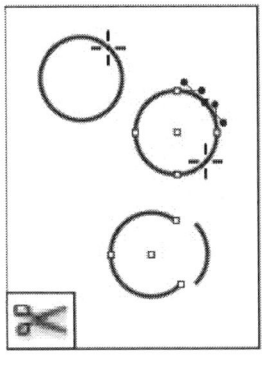

Tool: _____

Function: _____

Tool: _____

Function: _____

Tool: _____

Function: _____

Technology over technique produces emotionless design.

— Daniel Mall

TYPOGRAPHY TIPS

SERIF TEXT WITH A SANS SERIF HEADLINE
Serif text is almost always the better choice for body text in brochure printing. Serif fonts are the ones that have little "feet" or lines jutting out from the end of each letter. Examples: Times New Roman, Georgia. Sans Serif fonts, like Arial and Gill Sans, work better as headlines because headline text is larger and sans serif fonts are hard to read at small sizes.

USE CONTRASTING STYLES
Using Serif and Sans Serif fonts for different elements is also recommended because similar typefaces don't offer enough contrast and will therefore cause a visual clash. Using two script fonts for a headline and subheads won't work because there isn't enough of a difference for readers to tell which is a headline, and therefore a new subject, and which is a subhead.

DON'T USE TOO MANY FONTS
A lot of people are font happy. Just because their computer comes with 100 fonts, they feel as though they need to use each one in a single brochure. Fight this urge! Limit your number of fonts to three or four (two is actually preferred – one Serif and one Sans Serif) so that your brochure has a consistent look throughout. Changing from one font to another to another can make a brochure look like it's from multiple companies instead of one company trying to forge a brand message.

THE TEXT SHOULDN'T BLEND IN WITH THE BACKGROUND
Use dark text on a light background to ensure readability. You can use white on a black background, but it's harder on the eyes when the background is darker than the text. Just make sure not to use a light color like yellow on a light background, like light green.

SIZE
Set body text in 9-12 pt. type.
The leading should be 2-5 points higher than the font size.

CAPTION TEXT
- Set captions in a different typeface.
- Vary the weight of captions rather than making them too small (for instance setting captions in italics rather than 6 pt. type.)
- After to the cover, captions are the most read portions of a brochure; they must be readable.

GENERAL TEXT GUIDELINES
- Use graphical dingbats like bullets to break up the text
- Minimize the use of caps, italics, and bold
- Consider using color to vary appearance and call attention to specific items
- Be consistent (set all headlines in one typeface and style, all captions in one typeface and style, and so on)

MASTER PAGES

⊕ A master is like a background that you can quickly apply to many pages. Objects on a master appear on all pages with that master applied. Master items that appear on document pages are surrounded by a dotted border. Changes you make to a master are automatically applied to associated pages. Masters commonly contain repeating logos, page numbers, headers, and footers. They can also contain empty text or graphic frames that serve as placeholders on document pages. A master item cannot be selected on a document page unless the master item is overridden. (Ctrl + Shift on selected item overrides the master page)

⊕ Masters can have multiple layers, just like pages in your document. Objects on a single layer have their own stacking order within that layer. Objects on a master page layer appear behind objects assigned to the same layer in the document page.

⊕ If you want a master item to appear in front of objects on the document page, assign a higher layer to the object on the master. A master item on a higher layer appears in front of all objects on lower layers. Merging all layers will move master items behind document page objects.

Tips and guidelines for masters

⊕ You can compare alternative design ideas by creating a variety of masters and applying them in turn to sample pages containing typical content.

⊕ To quickly lay out new documents, you can save a set of masters in a document template, along with paragraph and character styles, color libraries, and other styles and presets.

⊕ If you change column or margin settings on a master, or apply a new master with different column and margin settings, you can force objects on the page to adjust to the new layout automatically.

⊕ Automatic page numbers inserted on a master display the correct page number for each section of the document to which the master is applied.

"To design is to communicate clearly by whatever means you can control or master."

— Milton Glaser

PAGINATION

You can add a current page number marker to your pages to specify where a page number sits on a page and how it will look. Because a page number marker updates automatically, the page number it displays is always correct—even as you add, remove, or rearrange pages in the document. Page number markers can be formatted and styled as text.

Page number markers are commonly added to master pages. When master pages are applied to document pages, the page numbering is updated automatically, similar to headers and footers.

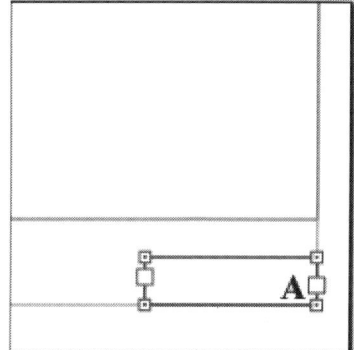 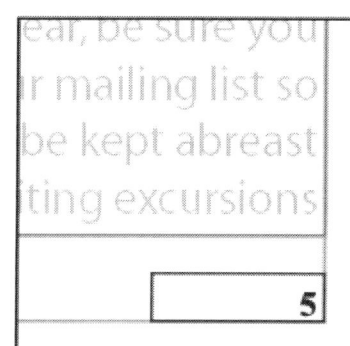

Page number on master A (left) and page 5 based on same master (right)

Add basic page numbering

⊕ In the Pages panel, double-click the master page to which you want to add your page number.

⊕ Create a new text frame large enough to hold the longest page number and any text you want to appear next to it. Position the text frame where you want the page number to appear.

If your document has facing pages, create separate text frames for the left and right master pages.

⊕ In the page number text frame, add any text that will come before or after the page number (such as "Page ").

⊕ Position the insertion point where you want the page number to appear, and then choose Type > Insert Special Character > Markers > Current Page Number.

⊕ Apply the master page to the document pages on which you want the page numbering to appear.

"If you want to make an apple pie from scratch, you must first create the universe."
— Carl Sagan

quick review! WORKING WITH STYLES

IF YOU HAVE A PLUS SIGN NEXT TO A STYLE, IT MEANS THAT THE STYLE HASN'T BEEN APPLIED 100% OR YOU CHANGED THE STYLING OF THAT TEXT. WHAT DO YOU DO:

1. Ignore: this is if you decide that in this place you want the text to look different there.
2. Alt Click on the style in the paragraph style panel: this brings it back to the original style it force applies
3. Redefine the style: shift+control+alt+r on the style makes your changes into the new style and it will change wherever the style is applied.

Paragraph style: controls all the styling including spacing and indents.
Character Style: overrides the paragraph style and it only formats character options.
Other: drop caps or when the first letter is a different font.

TO CREATE DROP CAPS:

Step 1: create your drop cap using your paragraph formatting options. I chose to do mine 3 lines, in a different font and color than the paragraph.

Step 2: Select just the drop cap, go to your character styles, create a new style (by clicking on the icon on the bottom that looks like you are turning a page)

Step 3: Create a new paragraph style and go to "drop caps and nested styles" choose how many lines you want your drop cap to be and the character style you created before.

Step 4: use it!

WORKING WITH NEXT STYLES & OBJECT STYLE

quick review!

1. Create your dropcap body style, title style and body style.
2. Double click on Title Style and choose the dropcap body style as the "Next Style"
3. Double click on dropcap body and choose the body style as the "Next Style"
4. Create another page in your document and place your "Ten Plagues" file.
5. Click on the text frame with your selection tool, give it a fill (you can lower the tint) and a stroke,
6. Right on your text frame and choose "text frame options" and after that choose inset spacing.

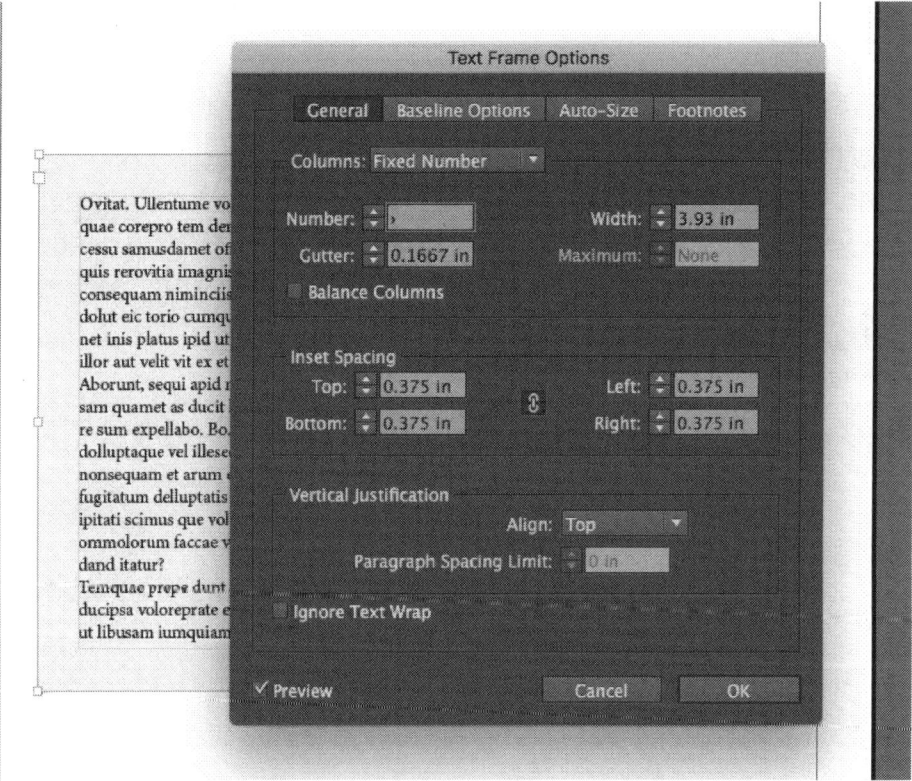

7. Go to your object styles and create a new object style of your text frame.
8. Make sure to check off paragraph styles and to choose Title as your first style and then check off next style.

quick review!
CREATE YOUR STYLES FOR YOUR PLAGUES BOOK

1. Put your cursor in your Title (Blood) and then go to your paragraph styles and click on the option "create a new" the icon looks like we are turning a page.
2. Click on your body text (if you have a drop cap, click on the paragraph without the drop cap- you may need to create a paragraph with no drop). Create a new style call it "body text without a drop cap".
3. Select your first letter- the dropcap and reate a character style of the drop cap. Name it "Drop Cap"
4. Click on your body text with the drop cap. Create a new style call it "body text with a drop cap". The style should be based on "body text without a drop cap", and at the side of the panel select "Drop Caps and Nested options" and choose the character style you created earlier called "Drop Cap"

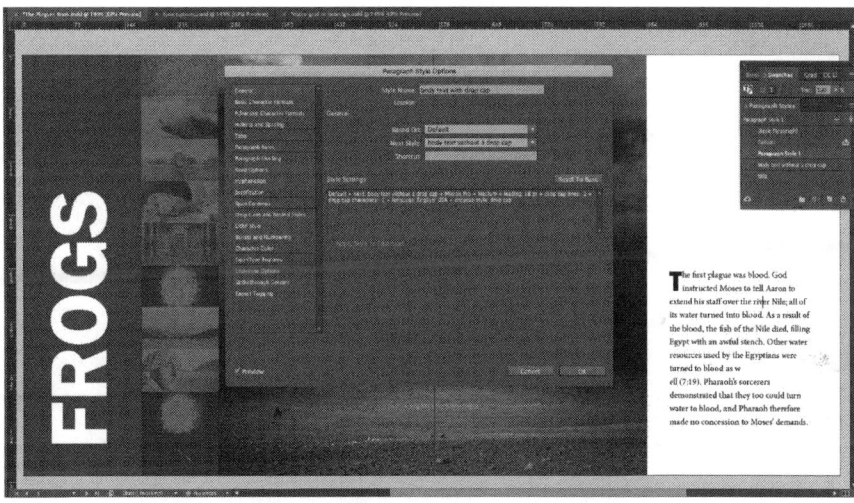

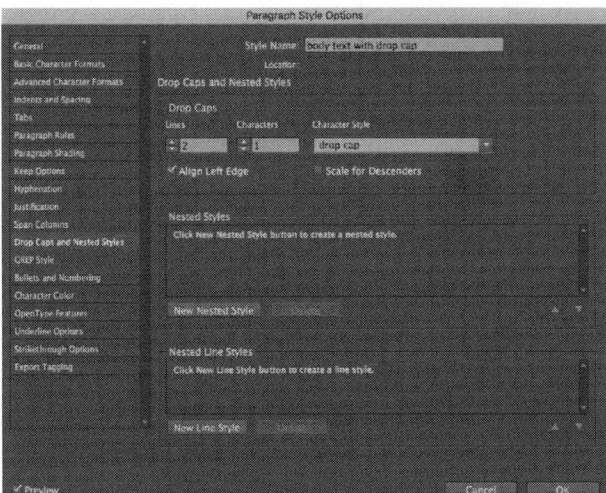

quick review!
SET UP YOUR MASTER & FLOW YOUR TEXT

PLACE YOUR OBJECTS ON YOUR MASTER PAGE:
1. Go to your spread that you designed
2. Select All (control+A)
3. Cut (control+X)
4. Click on your Master Page A (there's a line in your pages panel to get there)
5. Paste in Place (shift+control+alt+v) or edit paste in place
6. Since your Styles are SET, you click with your type tool inside your text frame, control+a to select all the text and delete it.
7. If you have a photo in your frame, double click on your frame to delete the content.

BRING IN AND THREAD YOUR TEXT:
1. go to page 2 in your booklet
2. file>place and choose the text for your document
3. hold down shift (to auto-flow) and click
4. click with your type tool inside your text frame, control+a to select all the text
5. Apply the paragraph style of your body text
6. Apply your title styles as appropriate (the first spread it the intro "the plagues")
7. after each plague is done, right click>insert break character> page break
8. every often when you get the + sign, click on the + hold down shift and then click on the text frame on the next page.

TROUBLESHOOTING:
If indesign isn't recognizing your text frame, it might be because it's too busy. select your text frame and cut it and paste it on a new layer, then you can lock your first layer and it should work.

PHOTOSHOP TOOLBOX

The toolbox contains the main tools for designing. Click any tool to select and use it.

A small arrow next to a tool in the toolbox indicates that the tool also has additional options available. In Photoshop, click and hold your mouse on a tool to see its options. For example, if you click and hold on the select tool, you'll see select options such as eliptical selction, single row selection, etc.

Tool Options
When you select a tool, additional options appear in the Tool Options bar (by default this is located just below the main menu).

Tools Panel Overview

A Selection tools
- Move (V)*
- Rectangular Marquee (M)
- Elliptical Marquee (M)
- Single Column Marquee
- Single Row Marquee
- Lasso (L)
- Polygonal Lasso (L)
- Magnetic Lasso (L)
- Quick Selection (W)
- Magic Wand (W)

B Crop and Slice tools
- Crop (C)
- Perspective Crop (C)
- Slice (C)
- Slice Select (C)

C Measuring tools
- Eyedropper (I)
- 3D Material Eyedropper (I)
- Color Sampler (I)
- Ruler (I)
- Note (I)
- Count (I)

D Retouching tools
- Spot Healing Brush (J)
- Healing Brush (J)
- Patch (J)
- Content Aware
- Red Eye (J)
- Clone Stamp (S)
- Pattern Stamp (S)

- Eraser (E)
- Background Eraser (E)
- Magic Eraser (E)
- Blur
- Sharpen
- Smudge
- Dodge (O)
- Burn (O)
- Sponge (O)

E Painting tools
- Brush (B)
- Pencil (B)
- Color Replacement (B)
- Mixer Brush (B)
- History Brush (Y)
- Art History Brush (Y)
- Gradient (G)
- Paint Bucket (G)
- 3D Material Drop

F Drawing and type tools
- Pen (P)
- Freeform Pen (P)
- Add Anchor Point
- Delete Anchor Point
- Convert Point
- Horizontal Type (T)
- Vertical Type (T)
- Horizontal Type Mask (T)
- Vertical Type Mask (T)

- Path Selection (A)
- Direct Selection (A)
- Rectangle (U)
- Rounded Rectangle (U)
- Ellipse (U)
- Polygon (U)
- Line (U)
- Custom Shape (U)

G Navigation tool
- Hand (H)
- Rotate View (R)
- Zoom (Z)

* Indicates default tool   * Keyboard shortcuts appear in parenthesis

"The real issue is not talent as an independent element, but talent in relationship to will, desire and persistence."
—Milton Glaser

selection tools
PHOTOSHOP TOOLBOX

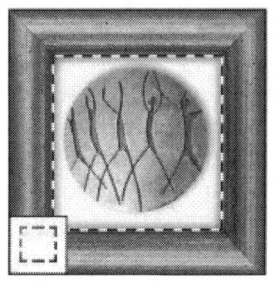

Tool: _____

Function: _____
_____

Tool: _____

Function: _____
_____

Tool: _____

Function: _____
_____

Tool: _____

Function: _____
_____

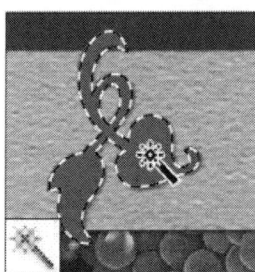

Tool: _____

Function: _____

Crop and slice tools

PHOTOSHOP TOOLBOX

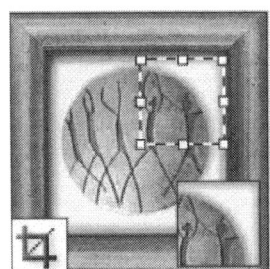

Tool: _____

Function: _____

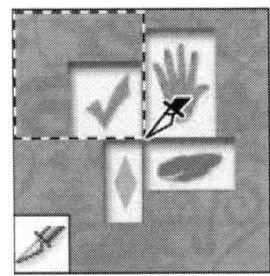

Tool: _____

Function: _____

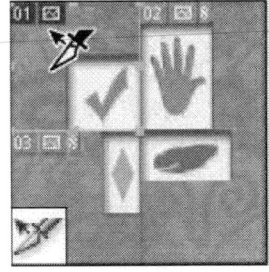

Tool: _____

Function: _____

Creativity is allowing yourself to make mistakes.
Design is knowing which ones to keep.

— Scott Adams

Retouching tools
PHOTOSHOP TOOLBOX

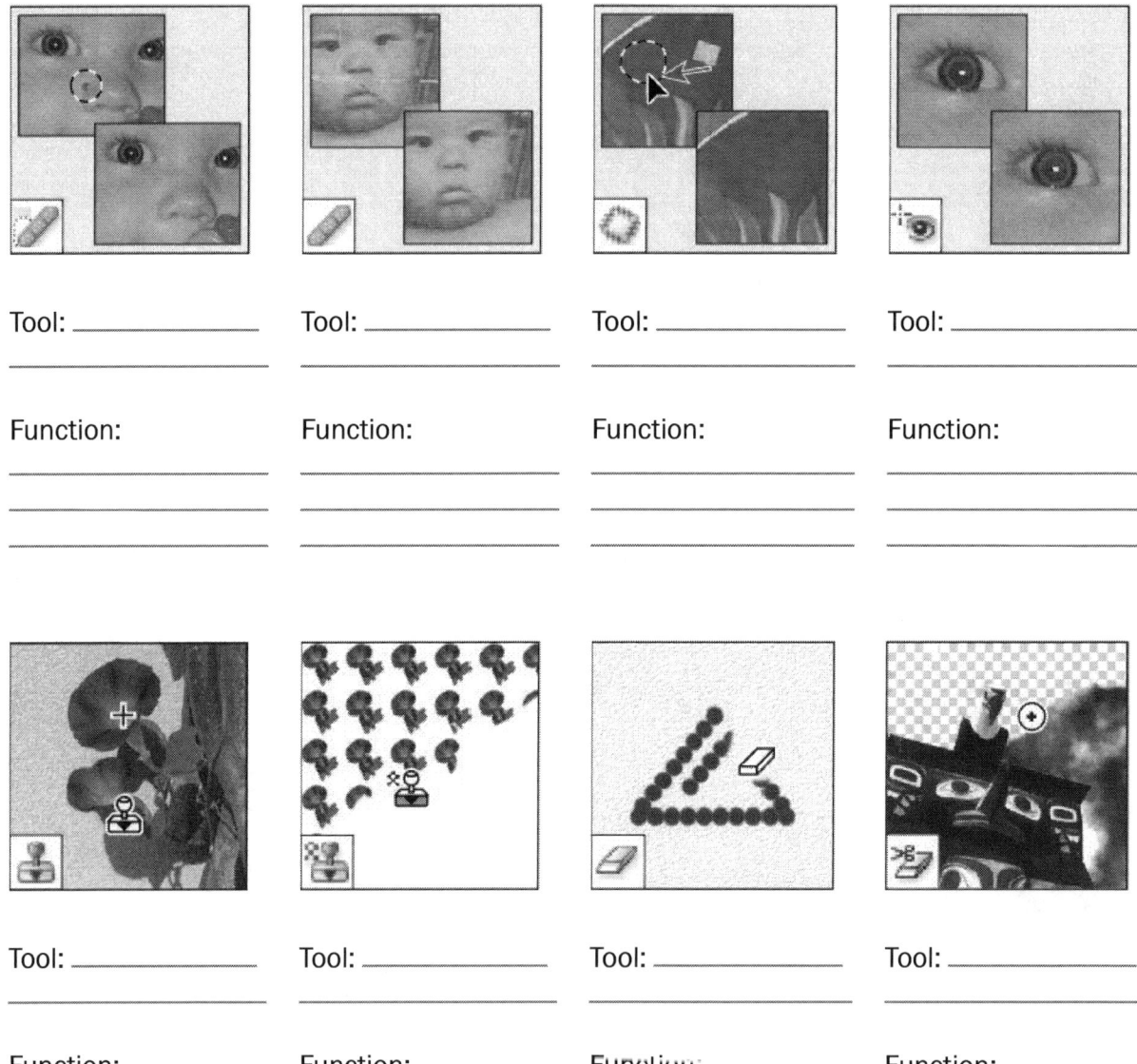

Tool: _____

Function:

Tool: _____

Function:

Tool: _____

Function:

Tool: _____

Function:

Tool: _____

Function:

Tool: _____

Function:

Tool: _____

Function:

Tool: _____

Function:

The ability to simplify means to eliminate the unnecessary so that the necessary may speak.

— Hans Hofmann

Retouching tools

PHOTOSHOP TOOLBOX

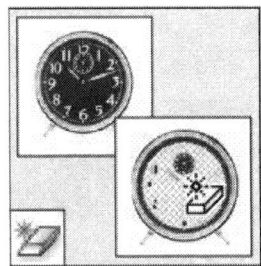 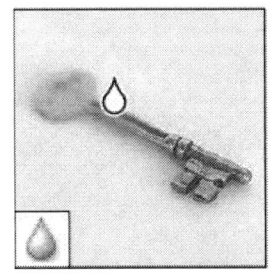  

Tool: _____

Function:

Tool: _____

Function:

Tool: _____

Function:

Tool: _____

Function:

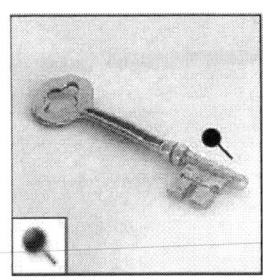  

Tool: _____

Function:

Tool: _____

Function:

Tool: _____

Function:

Genius is the ability to reduce the complicated to the simple.

— C.W. Ceram

Painting tools
PHOTOSHOP TOOLBOX

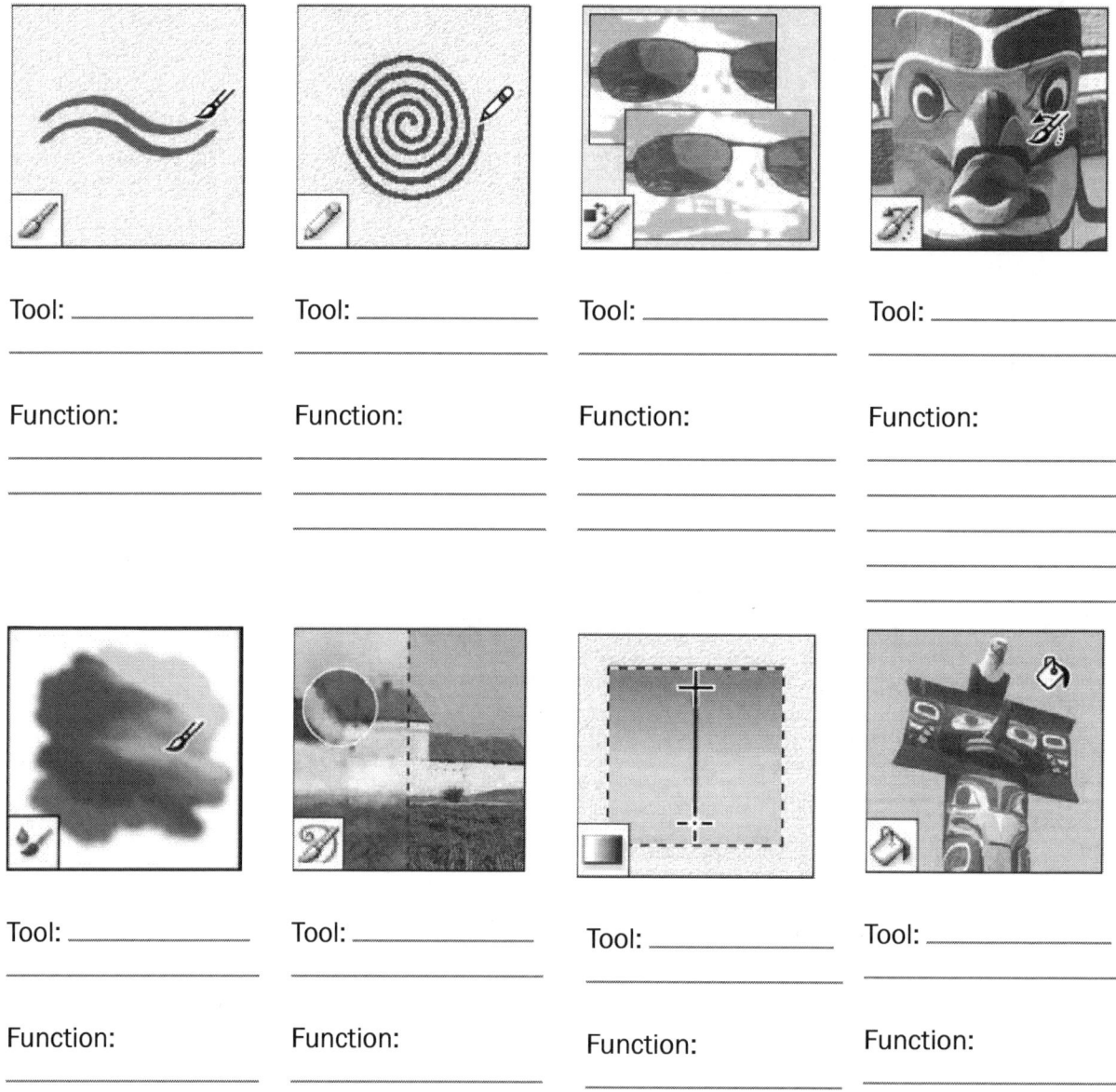

Tool: _____

Function:

Tool: _____

Function:

Tool: _____

Function:

Tool: _____

Function:

Tool: _____

Function:

Tool: _____

Function:

Tool: _____

Function:

Tool: _____

Function:

Drawing and type tools
PHOTOSHOP TOOLBOX

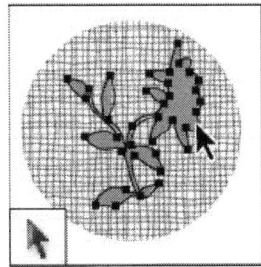

Tool: _____

Function:

Tool: _____

Function:

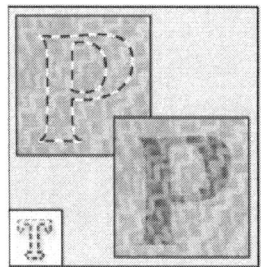

Tool: _____

Function:

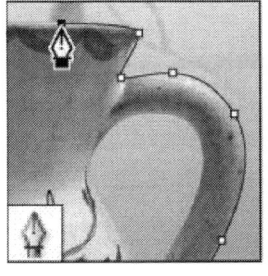

Tool: _____

Function:

Tool: _____

Function:

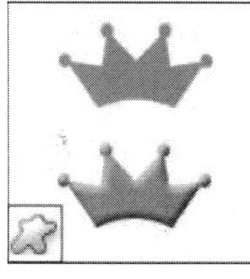

Tool: _____

Function:

> Designers may be the true intellectuals of the future.
>
> — Paola Antonelli

Annotation, measuring, and navigation tools
PHOTOSHOP TOOLBOX

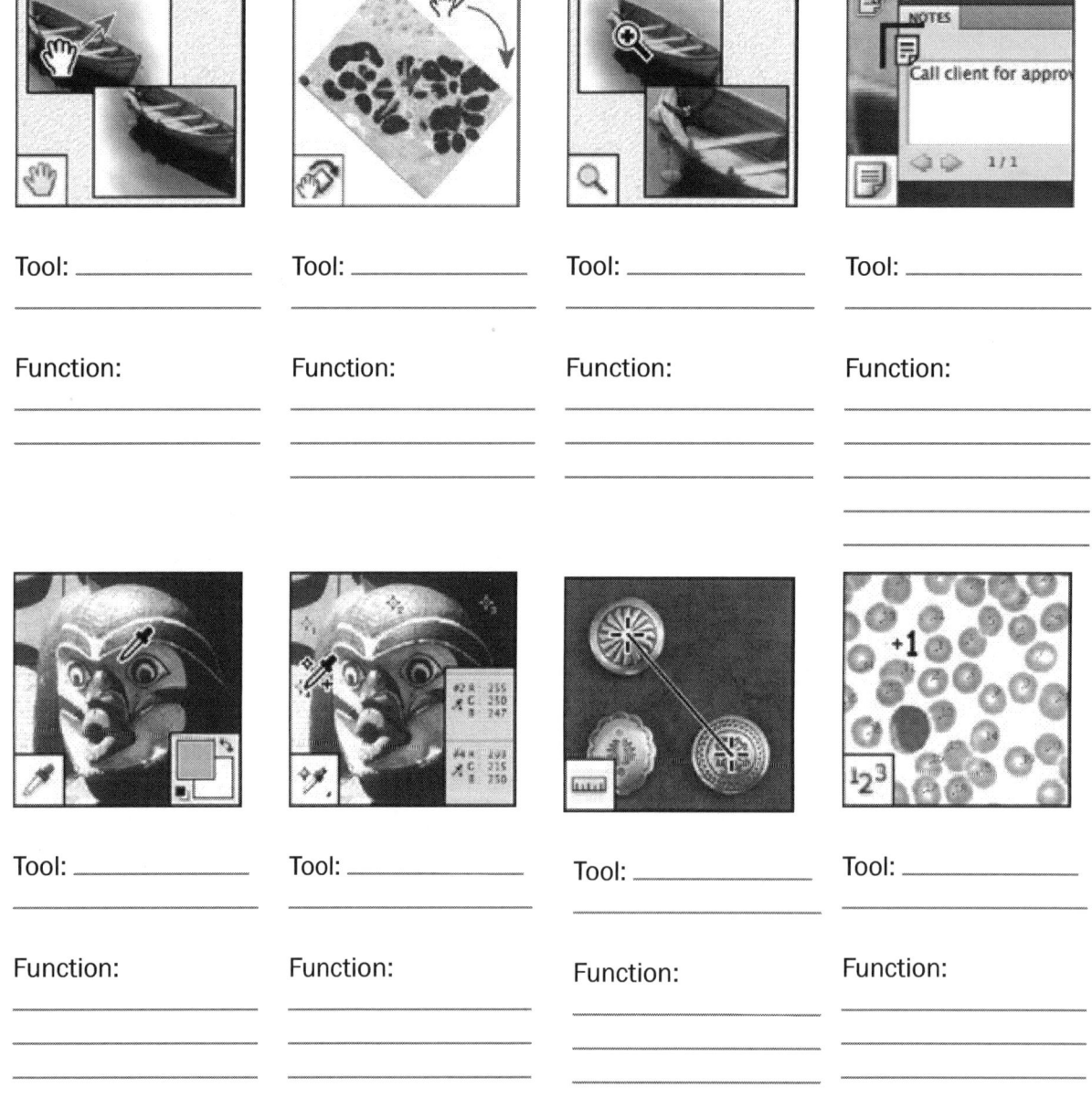

Tool: _____

Function:

Tool: _____

Function:

Tool: _____

Function:

Tool: _____

Function:

Tool: _____

Function:

Tool: _____

Function:

Tool: _____

Function:

Tool: _____

Function:

TRANSFORM

In Photoshop, Transform is used to scale, rotate, skew, and just distort the perspective of any graphic you're working with in general.

SCALING GRAPHICS

One of the most basic transformations Photoshop is capable of is scaling a graphic. Scaling allows you to enlarge or shrink a graphic around a reference point. To scale a graphic, we go to Edit > Transform > Scale. Or click on your move tool and check off "show transform controls"

A set of handles will appear around our selected elements in the document (such as layers, or shapes). By moving anyone of these handles, we can adjust the size of the object. To apply the transformation, hit Enter.

ROTATING OBJECTS IN PHOTOSHOP

Transform, but instead of dragging one of these, go just outside of the object until you see a curved arrow rotate icon. At this point, simple drag left or right to rotate the selected object. Once again, you must finish applying the transformation by pressing Enter.

REMEMBER:

- To transform proportionately you need to hold down the "SHIFT" key. (this depends on the version of photoshop you are using, it may be that you need to press shift only when you would like to distort)

- In order to apply the transformation you need to double click or press "enter"

TRANSFORM

The next 3 transformations are all similar, because they are all controlled by dragging handles. That is not to say that they are used to do the same thing, they simply all operate in the same manner. You can apply a Skew, Distort, or Perspective Transformation from Edit > Transform.

SKEW
Skew transformations slant objects either vertically or horizontally.

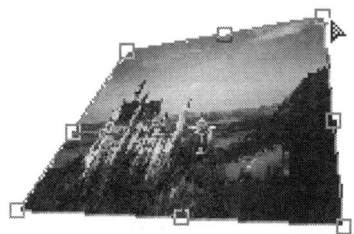

DISTORT
Distort transformations allow you to stretch an image in ANY direction.

PERSPECTIVE
The Perspective transformation allows you to add perspective to an object.

WARPING AN OBJECT
The Warp Transformation is quite a bit different compared to the other transformations. The entire shape of the object can be modified, making this transformation useful for several different effects. To use a Warp Transformation go to Edit > Transform > Warp. A Mesh will appear over your object that you can adjust by dragging control points, lines, or any other area inside of it. You can additionally apply a preset warp from the options bar.

PUPPET WARP

source: www.macworld.com

Puppet Warp overlaps your image with a mesh that you manipulate with control pins. Open any image in Photoshop, choose Layer -> New -> Layer From Background and then choose Edit -> Puppet Warp.

Your image will remain unchanged at this point, but you'll notice that a number of new items have appeared in the Options Bar. Click the checkbox to Show Mesh, and a gray mesh will be overlaid across your image. Choose More Points from the Density pop-up menu to double the mesh density, which will increase the accuracy of your warp. Now uncheck the option to Show Mesh, as we don't want it getting in the way.

Popping in control pins is easy—just click the image in an appropriate spot and a yellow circle will appear. It's important to note that pins function both as control points and point locks, meaning that if you don't want part of an image to be warped, you should add control pins to that area of the image to pin it into place. After you've laid down your pins, you can click any pin to select it (indicated by a black circle inside the yellow circle), and then drag it wherever you want. You can also delete any pin by selecting it and then tapping delete on your keyboard. Once you're happy with your warp, simply press return to lock it in.

BENDING OBJECTS WITH PUPPET WARP

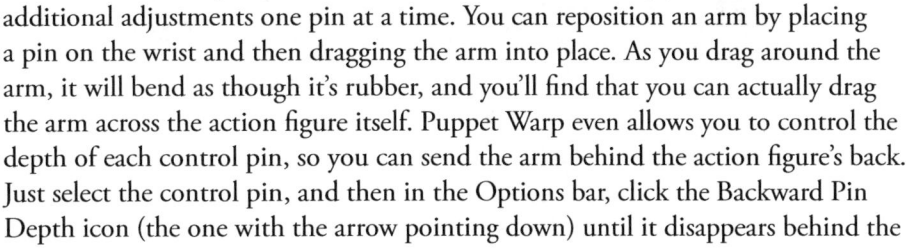

In order to bend objects freely with Puppet Warp—whether it's an action figure, a long-stem flower or a shoestring—the object must be cut out of its original picture and placed into a layer on its own. That is beyond the scope of this article, but you can learn how to do this in An Introduction to Masking.

After you've isolated your object on a new layer—in this example, we're using an action figure—choose Edit -> Puppet Warp and then click the checkbox to Show Mesh. You?ll notice that the mesh now covers only the object itself, and not the entire image. As before, you'll want to increase the mesh density by choose More Points from the Density pop-up menu, and then toggle the mesh visibility so that it doesn't get in the way.

First, lay down pins to lock areas into place (i.e., head, torso, and shoulder/hip joints), and then make additional adjustments one pin at a time. You can reposition an arm by placing a pin on the wrist and then dragging the arm into place. As you drag around the arm, it will bend as though it's rubber, and you'll find that you can actually drag the arm across the action figure itself. Puppet Warp even allows you to control the depth of each control pin, so you can send the arm behind the action figure's back. Just select the control pin, and then in the Options bar, click the Backward Pin Depth icon (the one with the arrow pointing down) until it disappears behind the action figure.

You may notice that your results are a bit ropey, which may not be always seem natural for a more rigid object like an action figure. Instead of dragging limbs around, you may have more success rotating pins as though they were joints. As before, you'll want to start by laying down pins to lock key areas into place (head, torso, shoulders and hips). Now select a shoulder joint and press the option key; immediately, you'll see a circle appear around the yellow control pin. Click and drag around the pin to rotate the arm, and then move on. Add a point for the elbow and rotate the forearm, then add a point for the wrist and rotate the hand. Keep in mind that you can click and drag points at any time to fine-tune the positioning, and tapping return will always lock in your warp.

PHOTOSHOP BLEND MODES

The Blend Modes specified in the options bar control how pixels in two separate layers interact with and effect each other. It's helpful to think in terms of the following colors when visualizing a blending mode's effect:

The base color is the original color in the bottom layer.
The blend color is the color being applied by the upper layer.
The result color is the color resulting from the blend.

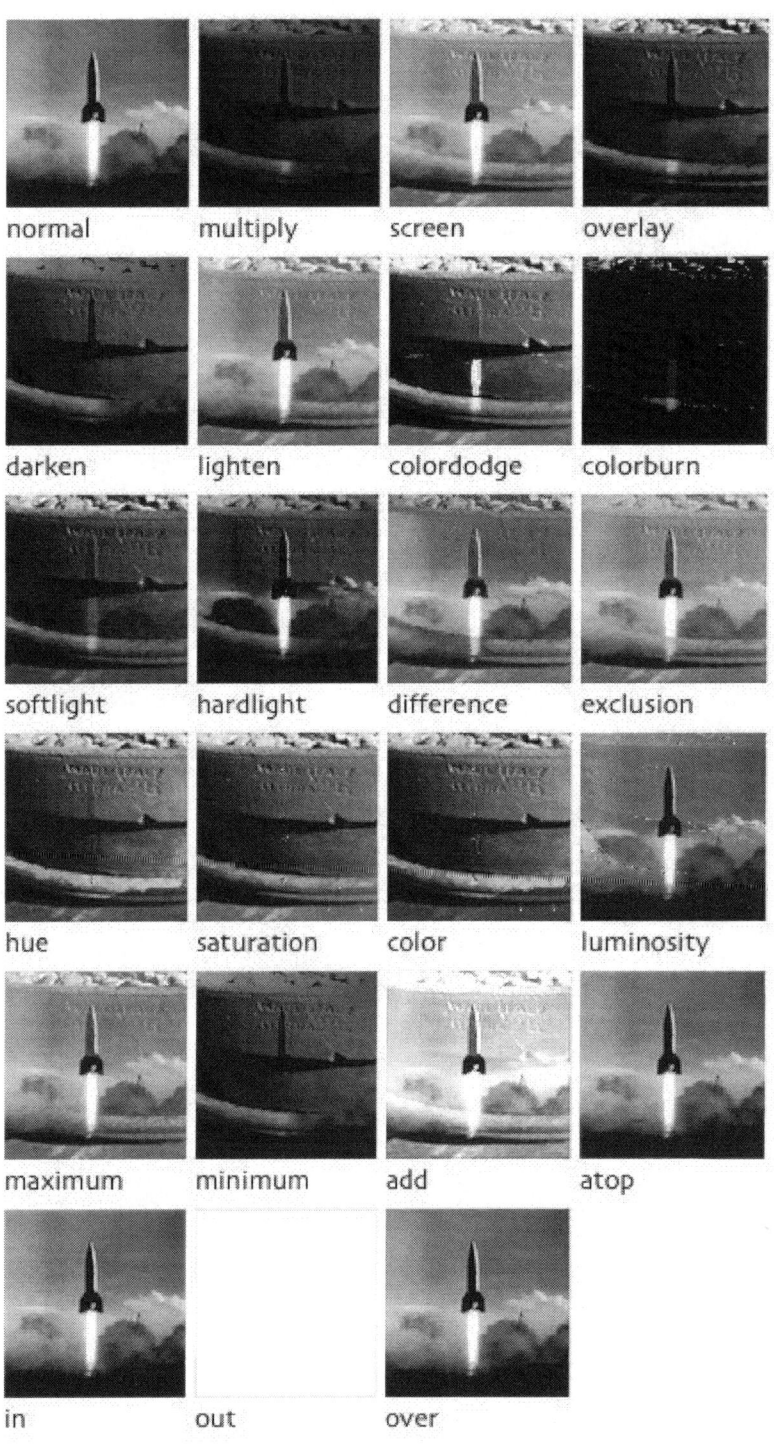

sources: psd.tutsplus.com and www.gfxcave.com

ADJUSTMENT LAYERS

This feature in Photoshop allows a designer or photo editor to non-destructively manipulate an image using various elements.

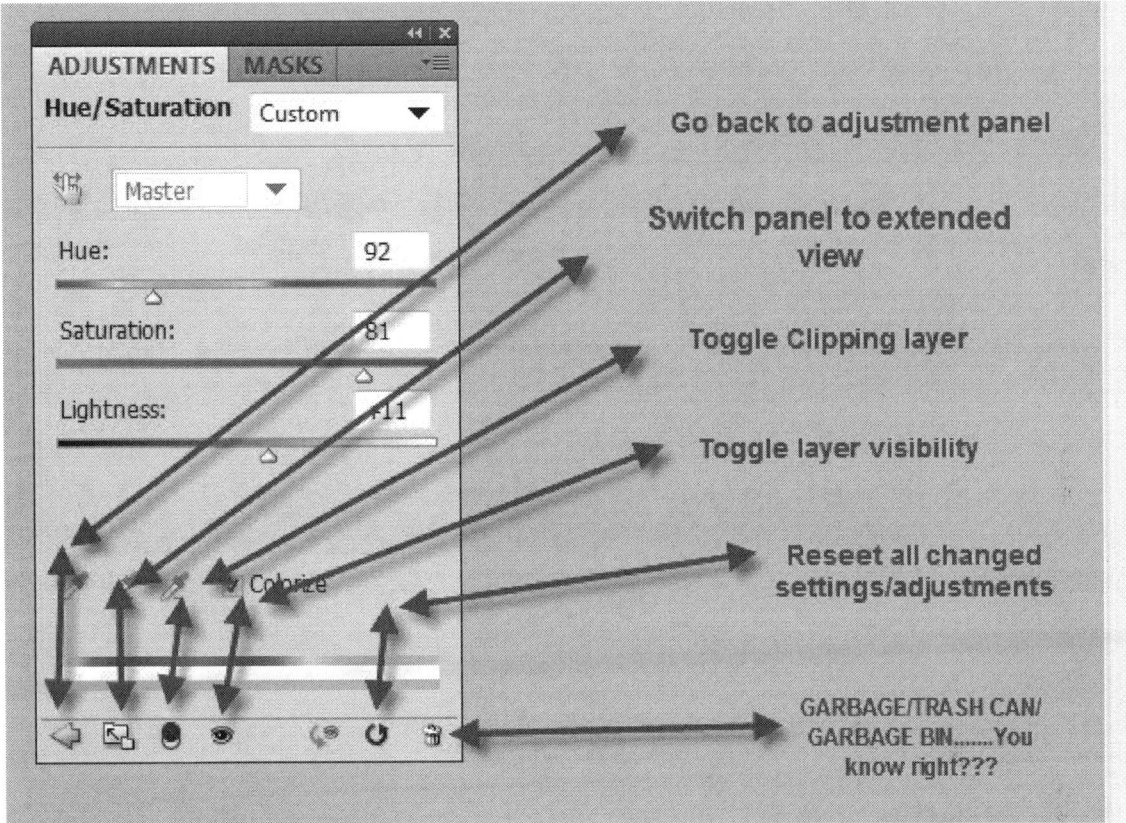

- Go back to adjustment panel
- Switch panel to extended view
- Toggle Clipping layer
- Toggle layer visibility
- Reseet all changed settings/adjustments
- GARBAGE/TRASH CAN/ GARBAGE BIN.......You know right???

Exposure
Before   After

THESE ARE THE OPTIONS THAT CAN BE FOUND WHEN AN ADJUSTMENT LAYER IS CURRENTLY ACTIVE AND BEING USED Many of the options highlighted above are very easy to use. You can simply "mouse over" an icon and you would get a simple text box with the name of the particular tool. Most of the icons are hard to learn at first but with constant practice it'll be very easy to identify an icon and know its use.

EXPOSURE

I mainly use exposure settings for brightening a photo. Basically, you can adjust highlights and shadows and everything in between without affecting one another. This is a smart way of lighting up a photo or for creating effects such as hdr. Although i forgot to depict it here, you can select the exposure settings by clicking the icon with the + and -................it is also the fourth icon on the adjustment panel.

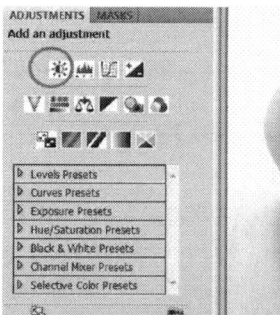

BRIGHTNESS/CONTRAST

Brightness and Contrast is used alot in photo editing and other general touch up procedures. As you can see from the pictorial explanations below, it is as easy as adding the adjustment layer and moving the slider to the right for brightness or to the left to darken an image. Contrast can be increased or decreased also by moving left or right. (right increases and left decreases).

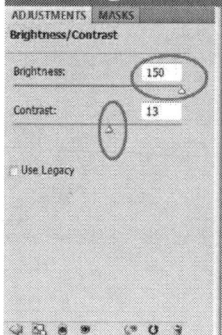

LEVELS

Lots of designers use this adjustment layers for adding a little contrast to images or brightening it up. With the levels adjustment layer you can edit the tonal range of an image by modifying the 3 different sliders. The black slider is used to adjust the tone of the shadows in an image, the grayish slider is for adjusting the tonal range of the mid-tones and the white is for adjusting the color tone of the highlights.

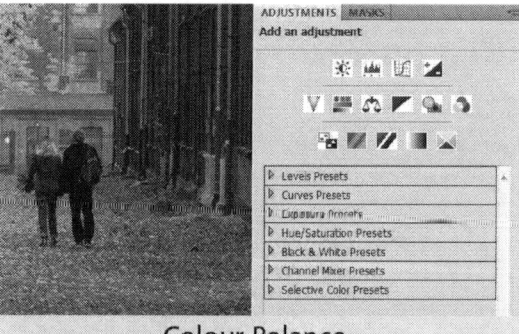
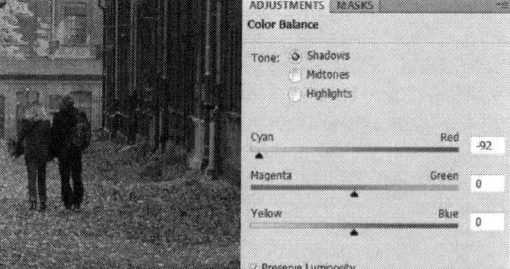

COLOR BALANCE

It seems like almost all these features have some similarities. You can use this to make small but generalized adjustments to colors in an image.

EYE DROPPERS

The black eye dropper is used to select a black point on your image and the white is used to select a white point on the image. Once you have used the eye droppers, your image colors would be automatically adjusted.

CURVES
With curves you can adjust as many tonal points as needed on an image. The range of the red, green and blue channels can be adjusted separately to get or achieve a desired effect. As in the images at the left, I over-edited them using curves just to depict the power of this wonderful feature.

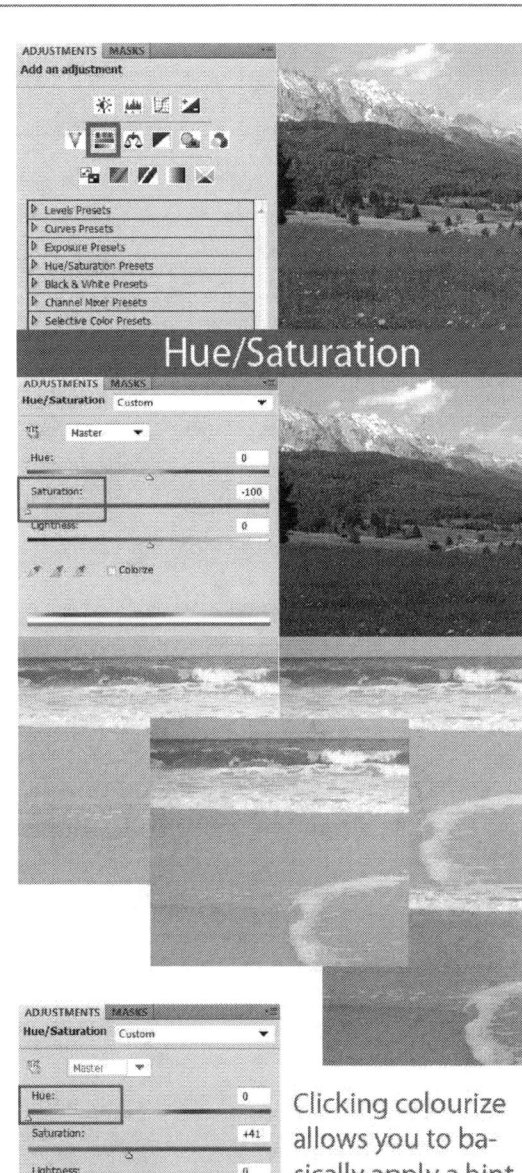

HUE/SATURATION
It can be used to increase/decrease the hue or saturation in an image. Most people i know, use it to create different tones for their images eg. sepia

Clicking colourize allows you to basically apply a hint of a particular colour over the image that the adjustment is applied to!

BLACK AND WHITE
Who doesn't love black and white. Almost every designer has created or used a black and white photo. Most people think that all black and white photos are the same, but simply adjusting the different colour values and properties can add some dramatics to your image. The icon for this feature is highlighted with the yellow square.

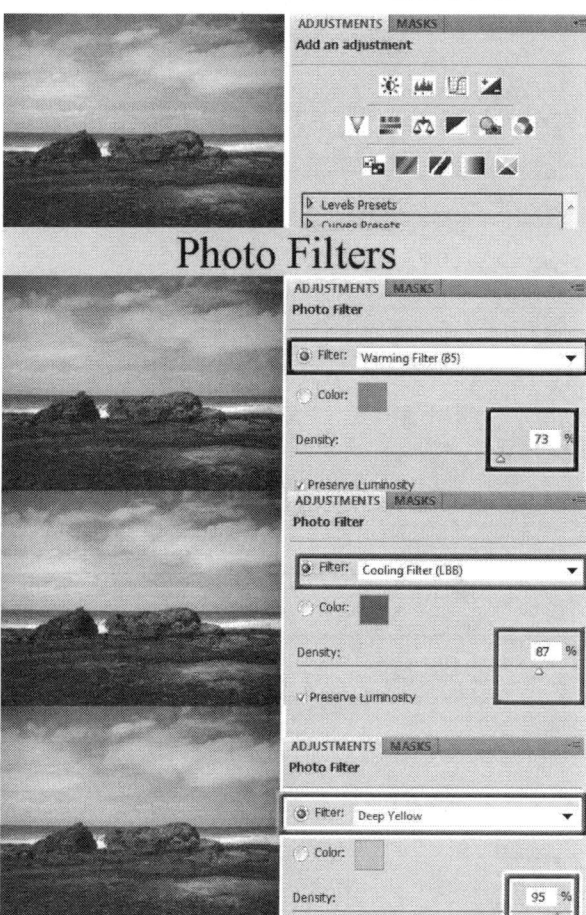

PHOTO FILTERS
Basically, a photo filter can be compared to placing a colored tint above your entire photo. Most designers i know, use these filters to blend an image together; because the color filter is one consistent tone, placing it above an image would make all the colors in the image have a hint of the color filter. The images above show the features of different photo filters.

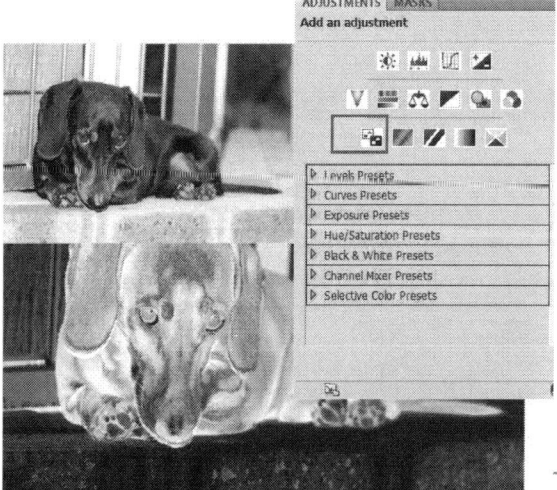

INVERT
Gives your image the "negative" effect.

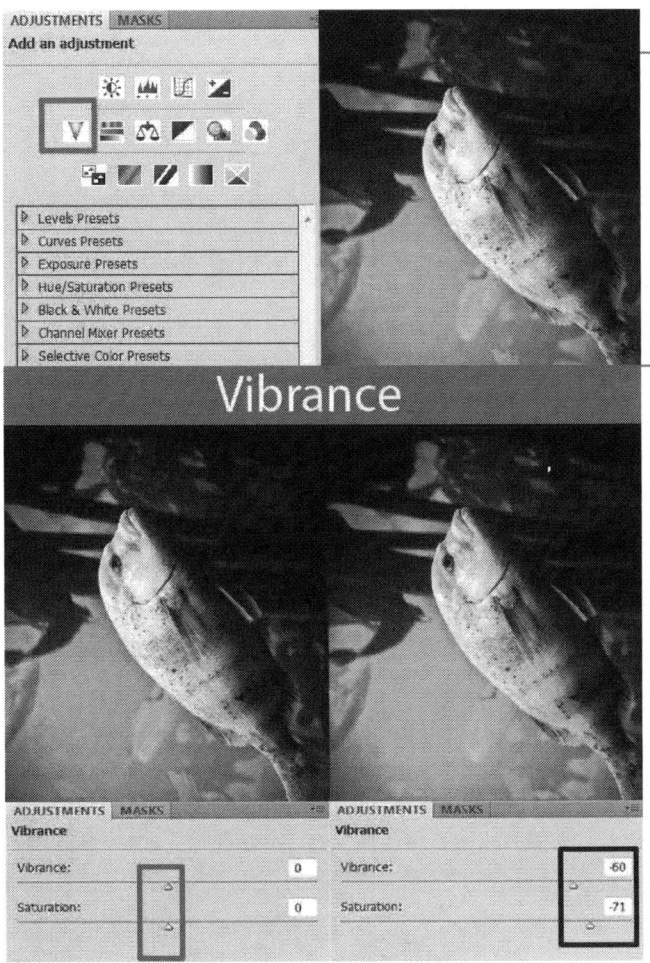

VIBRANCE

This filter can be used to increase the saturation levels in an image or make colors look brighter. It has varying functions which includes turning an image into black and white. The red box highlights the vibrance tool and the icon that is used to depict it.

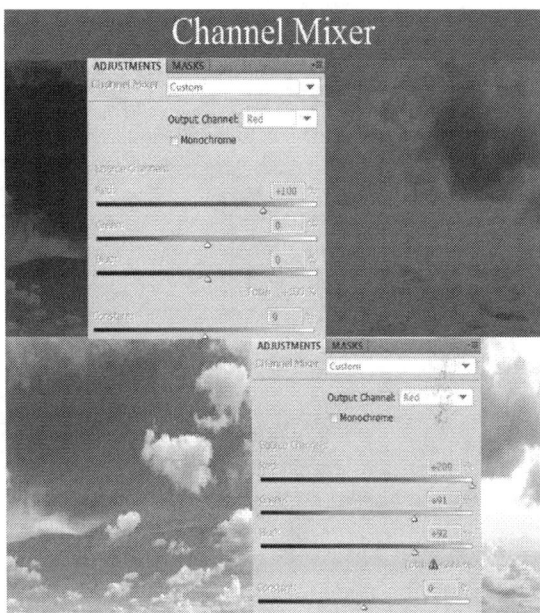

CHANNEL MIXER

We are going to use this beautiful image of clouds to demonstrate how the channel mixer feature works.

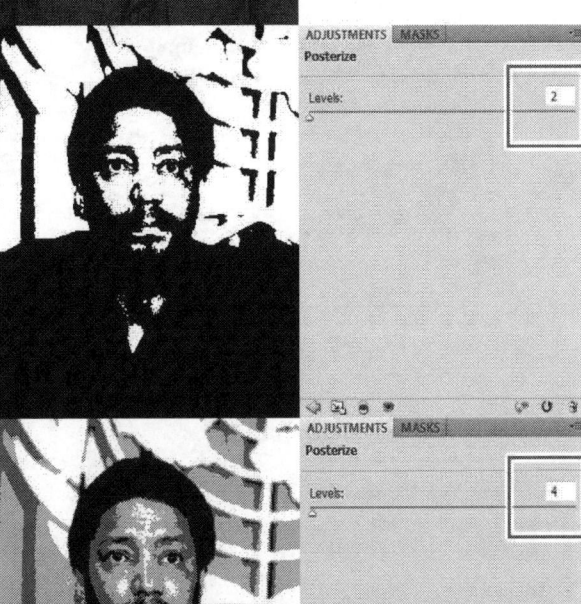

POSTERIZE

This effect is very popular amongst t-shirt designers. I know lots of people that use this effect for portraits and other fan arts of celebrities....I can't fully explain how important knowing about adjustment layers is to your design work. These simple tips and tricks is all that you need to start creating a masterpiece. (ROME Wasn't built in a day!)

Gradient Map

GRADIENT MAP
The simplest way of explaining this tool is that it basically overlays an image with a gradient. Therefore the highlights of image would be mapped by the higlights of the gradient and vice versa for the mid-tones and shadows.

Threshold

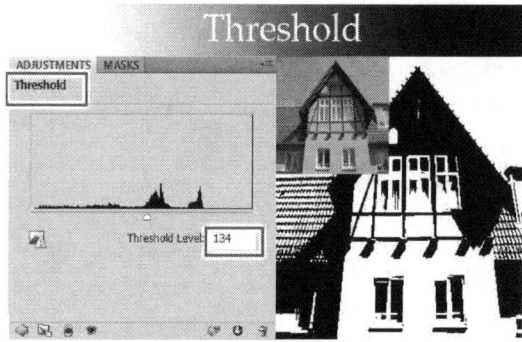

THRESHOLD
Threshold is similar to posterize. Many designers use this technique on t-shirt designs portraying famous personalities. With black and white photos it is almost impossible to tell the difference between a "posterized" photo or a "thresholderized" photo. (Thresholderized is not a real word, so use this term cautiously, lol)

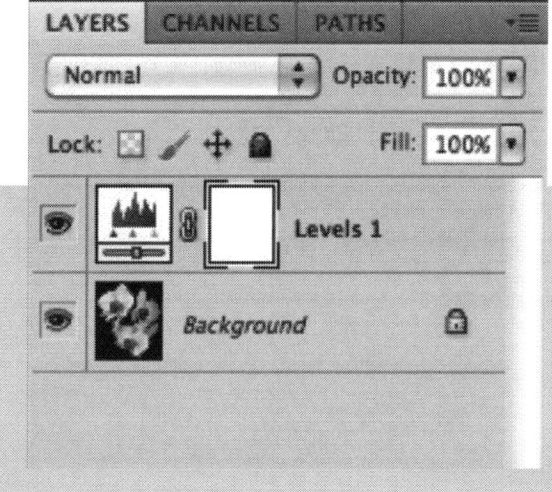

MASKING AN ADJUSTMENT LAYER

Do you recognize that white box on your adjustment layer?
Of course! it's a mask! You can apply the adjustment layer to some parts of your image and not to other's by masking it like you would mask any other layer. Just grab your paint brush and remember that back conceals and white reveals. In this case black will hide your adjustment and white will show it.

CREATE A CUSTOM PHOTOSHOP BRUSH

1 Ideally, If you want to make a brush that is "High-Res," you will need to set up your document that the brush will be 2500px in size.

You can use a color image to define a brush, but you might find it easier to convert your document to Grayscale in order to get a better idea of what to expect. When defining a brush preset, Photoshop will automatically convert your selection to grayscale to make the brush. White pixels will become transparent (which means you don't have to erase the white/background pixels! Keep reading below for details), Black pixels will be opaque, and everything in between will be see-through black/gray.

2 Make a selection around the area you want to use as a brush. Your selection cannot be feathered, and you cannot be selected the mask part of the layer.

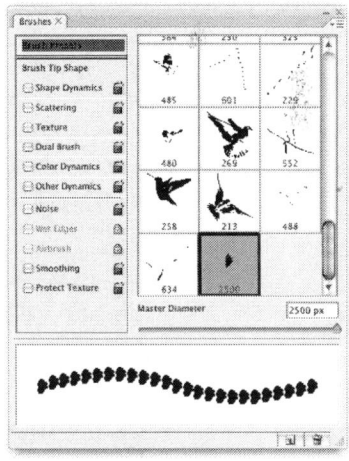

3 Go to Edit > Define Brush Preset.

PHOTOSHOP MASKS

Masks are incredibly useful for blending photos and hiding portions of images without altering them directly. When using a mask you do not delete or erase any part of your image. You just "hide" it, you can always get it back.

WHAT HAPPENS WHEN SOMEONE WEARS A MASK?

Dumb Question, yeah? It's obvious that everything behind the mask is not visible and everything else is visible. That's basically how Layer masks work except that you choose where the mask is and how opaque it is. Simple huh? So let's follow a quick tutorial. A Layer mask is just what it sounds like: a mask that goes on a layer. You can see through the holes but not through the mask itself. It's a great way to non-destructively hide parts of a layer. You will not lose any data and to go back to the original state you'll just delete the mask.

STEP 1: Find two images that you want to combine. Here are the images I used for the Frogs Plague:

BLACK = CONCEALS
WHITE = REVEALS

STEP 2: Open both the images in Photoshop. Then, choose the Arrow / Move Tool. Click on the frog image and drag it over to the image with the guy oven. You can resize the frog so that it's not too big or you can leave it the way it is. Your choice.

STEP 3: Choose the layer with the frog and then click on the Layer Mask button. It's the rectangle with the circle in it.
There it is! The layer mask. Currently it is set to reveal all of the image, meaning that the mask is off and nothing is hidden (since it is revealing everything!) That is why the box looks completely white. Now we actually use the mask.

STEP 4: Grab your PAINTBRUSH. Choose BLACK and start wildly painting. Paint over the leaves. Keep on painting until you only have the frog (you should use selection tools to assist you, select the section you want erased and then use the brush). Now what if you make a mistake and hide part of the frog? No problem. Layer masks are not destructive so just change the color to WHITE and paint over the glass and it'll magically reappear. You can basically adjust the brush size, or the shade of gray and you get way more control than using destructive methods. If you use an eraser you can't easily undo something you did 20 steps before etc etc.

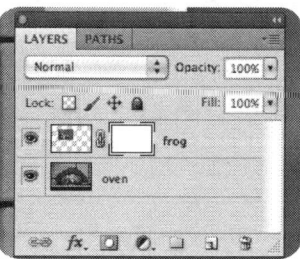

NOTES:

- You can go to Layer > Layer Masks > Reveal All or Hide All to apply the mask (also you can just choose the rectangle with the circle from the Layers window.)
- Use the "X" key to quickly switch between Black and White (to show and hide
- Shades of Gray in a layer mask change the opacity of the layer.
- A link icon appears in the middle of the layer and the layer mask. If it is linked then both the mask and layer can be moved together. If it is unlinked then you can independently move the layer and its mask.
- Be sure to click the Layer mask rectangle in the layer window when working with layer masks.
- Commonly, layer masks are used with Text and Gradients so experiment with those.

sources: photoshoptips.com and smashing magazine

Photoshop offers five methods of masking: Pixel Masks, Vector Masks, Quick Masks, Clipping Masks and Clipping Paths, all of which define pixel opacities without affecting the original data. Each of them has its own pros and cons, and knowing which method to use is extremely important for creating clean, flexible and properly masked layers.

Pixel Masks

Pixel masks determine opacity values based on a raster image with grayscale values that correspond pixel for pixel to the original layer. This makes them ideal for masking complex photographic imagery (e.g. the hair on a model or leaves on a tree). Pixel masks allow 100 shades of gray, which correspond directly to opacity percentages. The ability to vary opacities is unique to pixel masks, making them an invaluable tool.

While pixel masks can be easily modified, they aren't ideal for every situation. Because of their raster format, scaling them can cause unwanted artifacts and interpolated bluriness. Smooth curves and perfect edges can also be tricky to create when painting a mask. Under such circumstances, vector masks would be preferable.

ORIGINAL MASK   SCALED MASKS
Layer Mask   Vector Mask

CREATION

Creating a pixel mask is as easy as selecting the layer or layer group and clicking the "Add Layer Mask" button at the bottom of the layer's palette. A second thumbnail will be added to the layer, giving you a preview of the mask. By default, this will be entirely white. However, if you happen to have a selection active when creating the mask, the selection will be used to define the grayscale values of the mask.

Once a mask is created, it can be edited as if it were any other pixel data by clicking on the mask's thumbnail. You can then paint in black to hide areas or white to show them. The mask can also be tweaked using adjustments and filters such as Curves, Threshold, Unsharp mask and Gaussian blur.

VIEW MODES

While creating a mask, there are a number of ways to view the mask data. Option + clicking on the thumbnail will display only the mask on the canvas; this is great for fine-tuning areas but doesn't allow you to see the actual layer as you work. If you'd like to see both the mask and the layer at the same time, you can view the mask as a Ruby overlay. Simply press \ with the layer selected to toggle the overlay on and off. The color and opacity of the overlay can also be changed by double-clicking the mask's thumbnail. Additionally, if you'd like to temporarily remove the mask, you can toggle it on and off by Shift + clicking on the mask's thumbnail.

CHANNELS

Every time a layer with a mask is selected, the mask is shown as a temporary alpha channel in the Channels palette. From here, you can save the channel for later use by dragging the channel to the "Create new channel" button at the bottom of the palette or by selecting "New Channel" from the flyout menu. You can also change the mask's Ruby overlay settings by double-clicking the channel's thumbnail. Because a temporary channel becomes available whenever a masked layer is selected, you can use some keyboard shortcuts to toggle between the actual layer and its mask. Pressing Command + \ will select the mask and Command + 2 will bring you back to the layer data.

sources: photoshoptips.com and smashing magazine

Vector Masks

Vector masks pick up where pixel masks fall short. By defining the mask's shape using paths, vector masks provide a superior level of finesse and flexibility. They're ideal for defining shapes with clean, crisp lines, such as interface elements.

The disadvantage of vector masks is that they are unable to vary pixel opacities; they are basically either 0 or 100. For this reason, many masking jobs require a hybrid implementation. By using a vector mask to define the solid edges and a pixel mask for the more complex areas or for varying opacities, you can effectively extract objects while maximizing flexibility.

VIEW MODES
By clicking on the Vector Mask's thumbnail in the the Layer's palette, you can show or hide the paths saved in the mask. These paths can also be accessed from the Path's palette, but only if the layer itself is selected. Toggling the mask on and off can be done by Shift + clicking the thumbnail.

PATHS
Much like how layer masks appear in the Channels palette, a temporary work path would be displayed in the Paths palette when a layer with a vector mask is selected. You can then save the mask by dragging it to the "Create new path" button at the bottom of the palette or selecting "Save Path" from the fly-out menu. This temporary path can be accessed at any time by first selecting the Path Selection tool (A) and then pressing Enter; it can be dismissed by pressing Enter again. You can also quickly create a selection from an active path by pressing Command + Enter.

APPLYING
Before a vector mask can be applied to a layer it must first be rasterized by right-clicking the vector mask thumbnail and choosing Rasterize Vector Mask. If the layer already has a pixel mask, the two masks will be composited together to create a single pixel mask. It can then be applied like any other layer mask (right-clicking the thumbnail and choosing "Apply Layer Mask").

Quick Masks

The Quick Mask mode allows you to create a selection using pixel editing tools as opposed to the primitive selection tools. This is a more logical approach to creating a complex mask with variable opacity. You can access this mode by clicking on the "Quick Mask" button in the Tools bar or by pressing Q.

Once in Quick Mask mode, you'll no longer be editing the current layer. Instead, you'll be editing a Ruby overlay that can be edited as if it were regular pixel data. By default, entering this mode will cover the entire canvas with a semi-transparent red color. You can then paint white to remove the overlay and black to add it back. The Quick Mask is essentially a more visual representation of a selection. Therefore, every area that you remove from the overlay is added to the selection.

SAVING
After creating a quick mask, you can immediately apply it to a layer by creating a layer mask or save it for later use. By selecting Selection > Save Selection, you can save your selection as a new channel or apply it to an existing channel. This allows you to come back to the selection at any time by Control + clicking the channel in the Channel's palette or by selecting Selection > Load Selection

sources: photoshoptips.com and smashing magazine

Clipping Masks

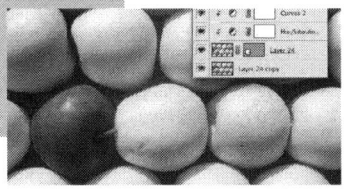

You'll often run into situations in which multiple layers require the same mask. You could group the layers and mask the layer group, but that is not always ideal. Clipping masks allows for a layer simply to adopt the opacity of an underlying layer. This is extremely helpful when using adjustment layers; by clipping them to a layer, you can apply adjustments to a single layer without affecting those below it.

The easiest way to create a clipping mask is to Option + click between the two layers in the Layer's palette when the clipping mask cursor appears. Alternatively, you could press Command + Option + G to clip a layer to the one below it. Any number of layers can be clipped to one master layer, but a clipped layer can't be used as a clipping mask itself.

Clipping Paths

Clipping Paths are a lot like Vector Masks except that they apply to an entire document rather than a layer or layer group. They are primarily used by print designers to specify uniquely shaped objects that are imported into a page layout program. The path is imported along with the image to ensure a crisp clean edge.

To create a clipping path, first be sure that you have a path saved; having a temporary Work Path does not suffice. You must select "Save Path" from the fly-out menu in the Paths palette if your path is not saved. Then, from the fly-out menu, choose "Clipping Path." Your document's appearance will not change, but if you were to import the document into Illustrator using the Place command, it would be clipped to the path

MASKS PALETTE

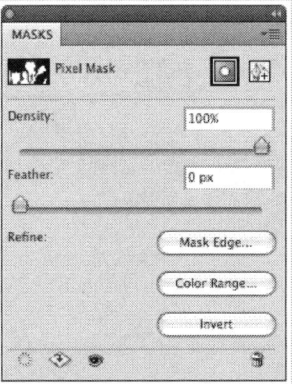

CREATE/VIEW BUTTONS At the top of the palette are two buttons that can be used to select the layer mask or vector mask or to create one if one doesn't exist.

DENSITY The density slider basically controls how strong the mask is. At 100%, fully masked areas will be completely transparent. When density is set to 50%, those same areas would be only 50% transparent.

FEATHER Feathering the edges of a mask used to require applying a Gaussian Blur, which would destroy the original mask shape. With the Masks palette you can now change the amount of feathering at any time while maintaining the original mask data.

MASK EDGE The Mask Edge menu provides some long-desired features that aid in refining a mask's perimeter. They come in extremely handy when the extracted object is still picking up color from the masked background.

RADIUS The Radius setting is similar to feathering, but it retains some of the edge's crispness. This can be helpful with reducing awkward or overly sharp edges on complex shapes.

CONTRAST Contrast simply modifies the contrast of edge elements, which helps crispen any soft edges. Using this in conjunction with Radius can help remove unwanted artifacts in the mask.

SMOOTH Smooth simplifies the complexity of the mask's edges. This can be useful if you've painted the mask by hand and need to quickly clean up some rough edges.

FEATHER This feather command is nearly identical to the Mask palette's primary feather command, but it restricts the blur more to the edge of the mask. The difference is slight yet noticeable.

CONTRACT/EXPAND The Contract and Expand slider allows you to grow and shrink the edges of the mask. This is extremely useful for reducing unwanted color fringes.

PREVIEW MODE At the bottom of the palette are five different preview modes that allow you to view the mask as a (1) selection with marching ants, (2) quick mask ruby overlay, (3) black matte, (4) white matte or (5) grayscale mask.

COLOR RANGE The Color Range menu is one of the most powerful ways to extract an image from an evenly colored background. With only a few clicks and adjustments, even the most complex object can be cleanly masked. For further details, see the "Techniques" section just below.

sources: psd.tutsplus.com and smashing magazine

PEN TOOL

The Pen Tool makes appearances across almost the entire Adobe product range. Its function and behavior varies depending on the application, but by mastering it youll find you work quicker, smoother and with better results.

Basic Pen

Click on the canvas to create paths with straight segments, click and drag to create paths with Bezier curves.

Add Anchor Point

Click on a path segment to add anchor point.

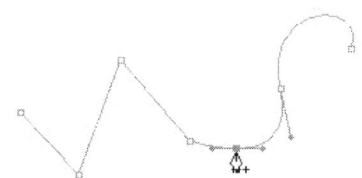

Delete Anchor Point

Click on anchor point to remove from path.

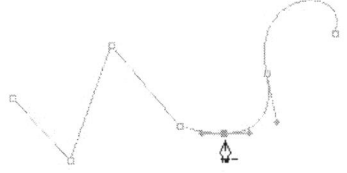

Convert Point tool

Click on an anchor point and drag to create bezier handles where there were none, click on an anchor point with handles to a remove them.

BÉZIER CURVE:

A Bézier curve is a parametric curve frequently used in computer graphics and related fields. Generalizations of Bézier curves to higher dimensions are called Bézier surfaces, of which the Bézier triangle is a special case.

In vector graphics, Bézier curves are used to model smooth curves that can be scaled indefinitely. "Paths," as they are commonly referred to in image manipulation programs,[are combinations of linked Bézier curves. Paths are not bound by the limits of rasterized images and are intuitive to modify. Bézier curves are also used in animation as a tool to control motion.

(source: http://en.wikipedia.org/)

Freehand Pen

Click on the canvas and drag to draw paths freely, as though using a brush.

sources: psd.tutsplus.com and smashing magazine

PEN TOOL OPTIONS TOOLBAR

The Options Bar (Window > Options), usually located at the top of your screen, provides the most important options for whichever tool is selected. This is also true of the Pen Tools and their options are outlined below.

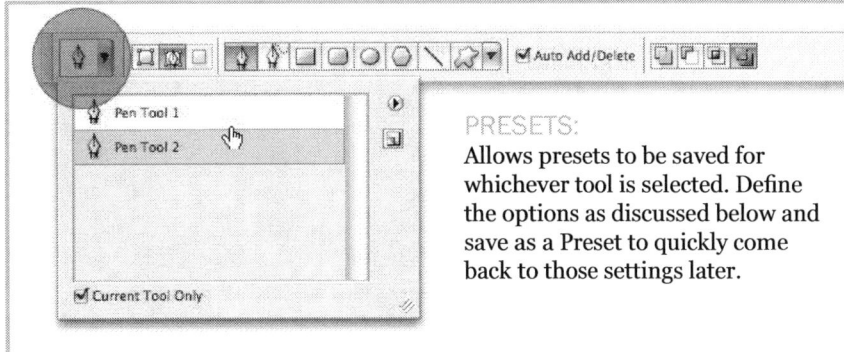

PRESETS:
Allows presets to be saved for whichever tool is selected. Define the options as discussed below and save as a Preset to quickly come back to those settings later.

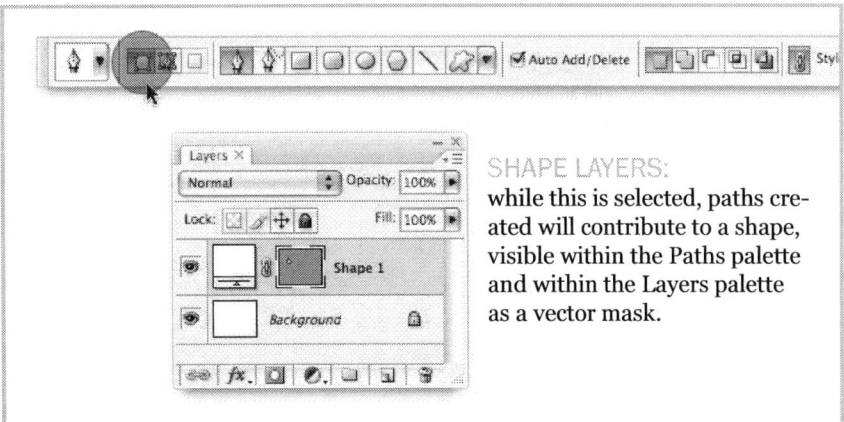

SHAPE LAYERS:
while this is selected, paths created will contribute to a shape, visible within the Paths palette and within the Layers palette as a vector mask.

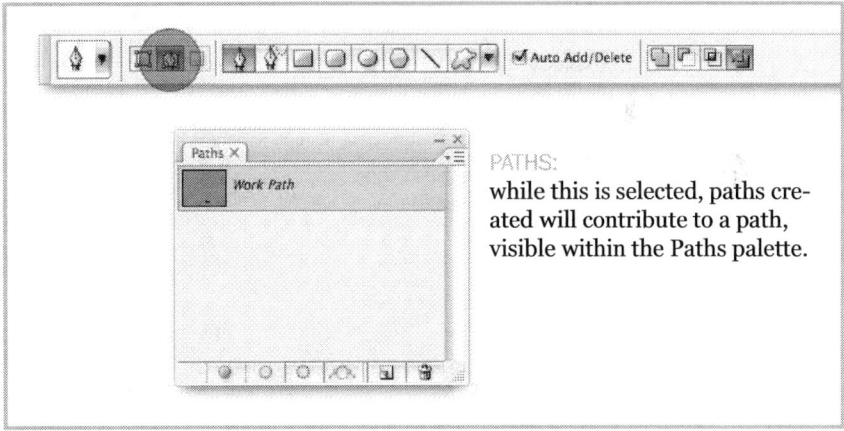

PATHS:
while this is selected, paths created will contribute to a path, visible within the Paths palette.

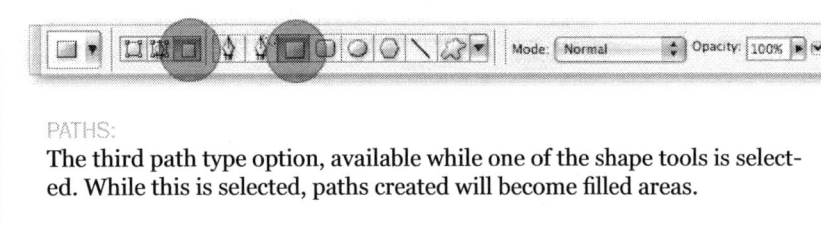

PATHS:
The third path type option, available while one of the shape tools is selected. While this is selected, paths created will become filled areas.

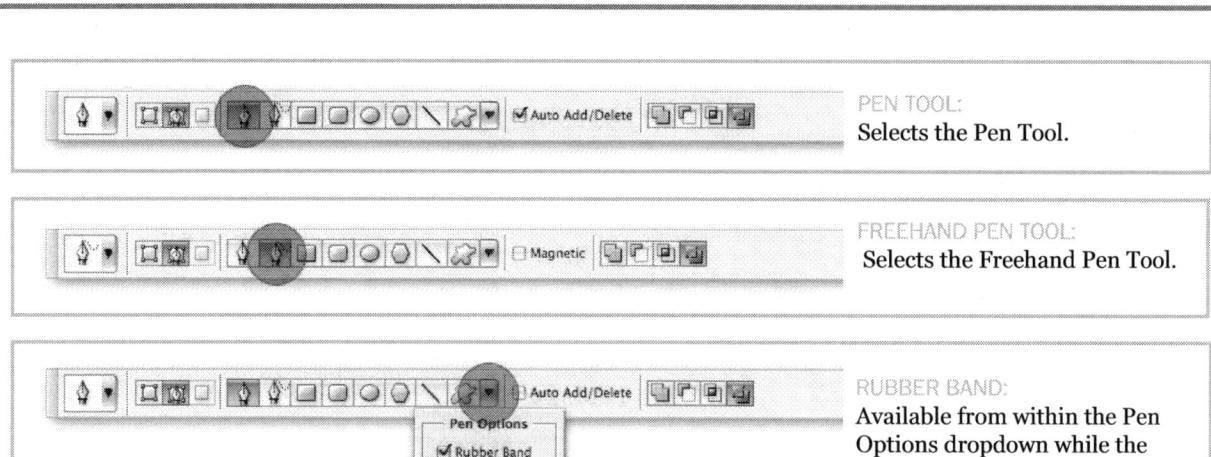

PEN TOOL:
Selects the Pen Tool.

FREEHAND PEN TOOL:
Selects the Freehand Pen Tool.

RUBBER BAND:
Available from within the Pen Options dropdown while the Pen Tool is selected. Rubber Band gives a visual of the path youre about to create, without you having the cursor pressed on the canvas.

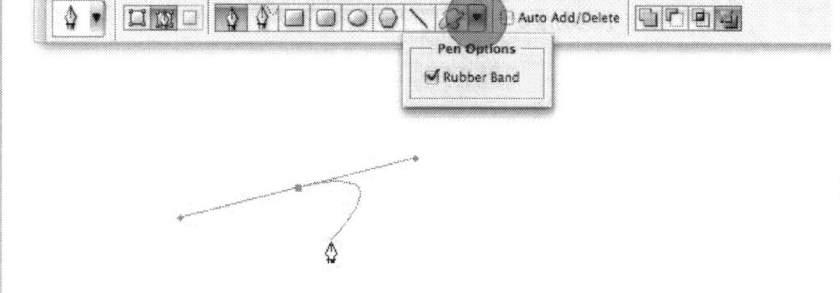

CURVE FIT:
Available from within the Freehand Pen Options dropdown while the Freehand Pen Tool is selected. Value entered determines the accuracy to which bezier handles will be added to your freely drawn path. The higher the value, the more accurate your result will be. A value of between 0.5 and 10 pixels is required.

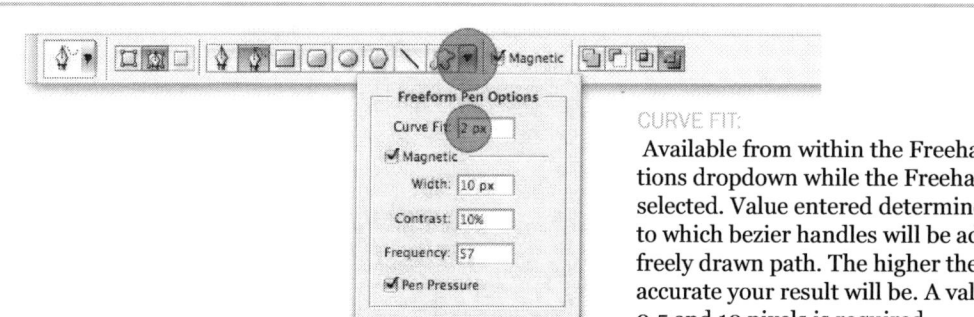

MAGNETIC:
Available from the Options bar and within the Freehand Pen Options dropdown while the Freehand Pen Tool is selected. When selected, paths drawn will magnetize to pixels. The Magnetic settings as shown below, determine the width of the area the path is prepared to jump across, the contrast of the pixels necessary to attract the path and the frequency of anchor points added to the path.

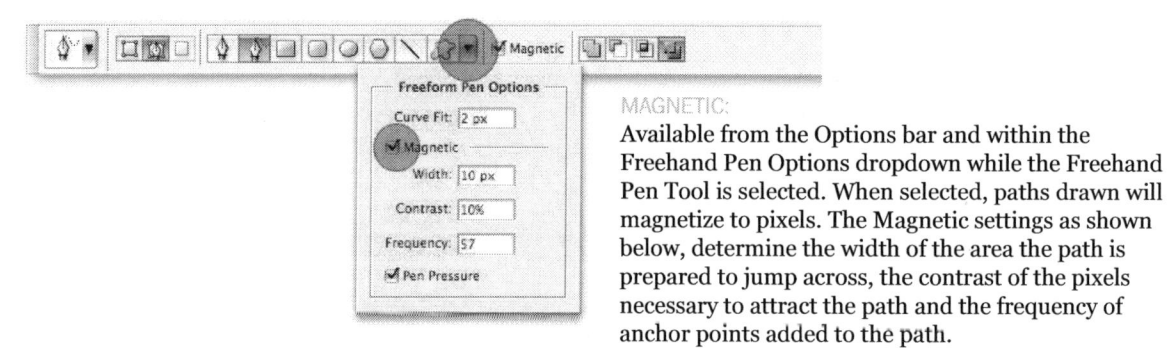

PEN PRESSURE:
When selected, the pressure applied to a graphics tablet (if youre using one) influences the pen width.

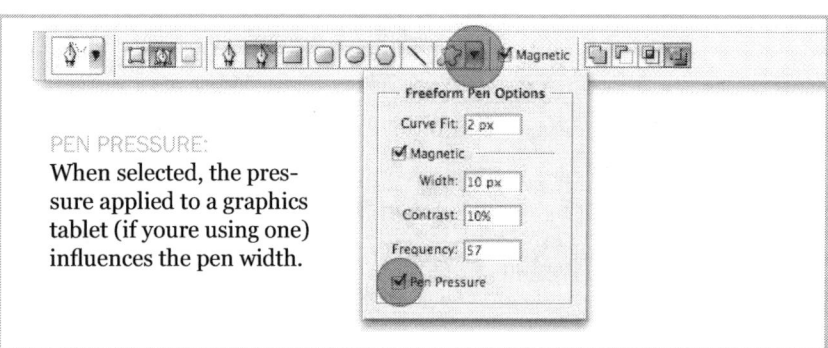

AUTO ADD/DELETE:
Allows adding and removing of anchor points with the normal Pen Tool.

PATHFINDER TOOLS:
These allow addition, subtraction, intersection and exclusion of the paths you create..

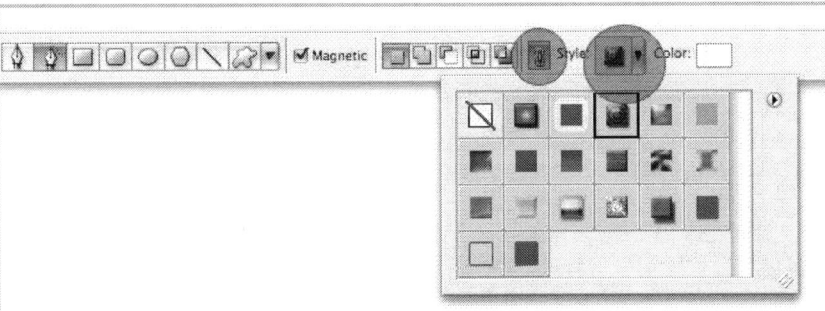

LAYER STYLE:
Available when Shape Layer is selected; this applies layer styles to shapes on a new layer (if chain link is unselected) or to shapes on the current layer (if chain link is selected).

Position anchor points on a curve where the paths begin to change direction, not in the middle of its curve.

Drag handles from the first anchor point when beginning a curved path.
Drag your handles around just one third of the curve youre creating for a smooth path.

This is all well and good in theory... The more you practice the better you'll get at it!

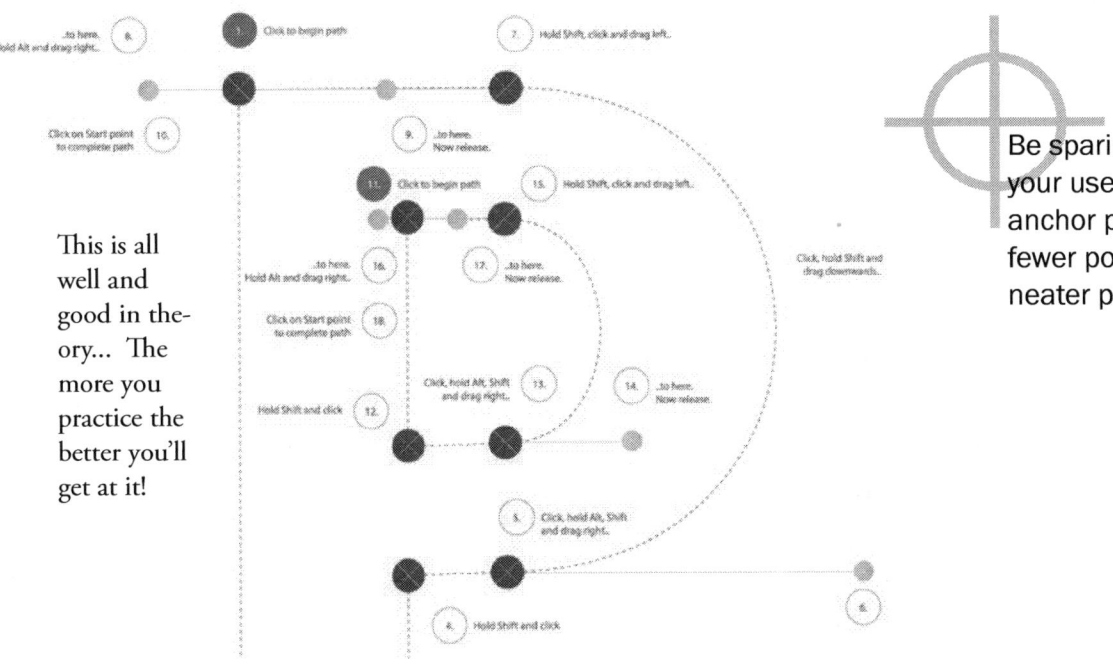

Be sparing with your use of anchor points, fewer points = neater path.

quick review!
MAKE GRID IN INDESIGN

1. Create the shape or bring in the photo that you want broken up into a grid.
2. Make sure that the object is selected.
3. Go to: Window>Utilities>Scripts
4. In Scripts: Click on the arrow to expand Application>Saples>Java Script> Make Grid. Double click on make grid.

5. Choose how many columns and rows you want and gutter is the space between them. Click enter and you are done!

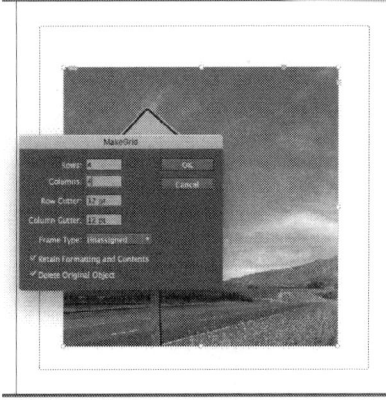

quick review!
PLAGUES WITH ADJUSTMENT LAYERS

DARKNESS:
1. Open the image that you want to use for darkness
2. Click on the black and white cookie at the bottom of your layers panel, choose an adjustment layer, "levels" might be a good choice.
3. In the adjustment layer properties panels that pops up you can play around with your options. For example you can drag the black house slider to the left to make the image darker. And you can drag the white house slider at the bottom to the left to make the general brightness darker.
4. File> Save as> darkness

BLOOD:
1. Open the image that you want to use for blood
2. Click on the black and white cookie at the bottom of your layers panel, choose an adjustment layer, "color balance" might be a good choice.
3. In the adjustment layer properties panels that pops up you can play around with your options. For example you can drag your controls from cyan to red, you should change your midtones, your highlights and your shadows.
4. did you notice that your adjustment layer automatically comes with a mask? click on the mask part of your layer and you can use your brush tool to mask, remember that black conceals and white reveals. Use your adjustment tools to assist you.

TIPS:
- You can also first make a selection and then click on your adjustment layer, whatever was selected will be part of your adjustment layer.
- If you have a small boat that you would like to get rid of, you can duplicate your background and use your patch tool to remove the boat.
- If you want to manipulate your adjustment layer, in your layer panel you can double click on the black and white cookie icon on the layer by the adjustment mode (not the icon at the bottom)
- You can layer adjustment layers.
- You can clip an adjustment layer to the layer under it by clicking "alt" between the layers. (similar to what we did with the flower and image clipping mask)
- If you are using more than one adjustment layer and you want them to have the same mask, you can create a group by clicking on your folder at the bottom of your layers panel and drawing the adjustment layers into the group, then you give the folder a mask and anything inside the folder will have that mask.

SMART OBJECTS
quick review!

WHAT IS A SMART OBJECT?
A linked file that photoshop is taking the info from.
It can be linked like an indesign file, or embedded within the psd file. (If you are using cs6 or earlier, you only have the embedded option)

WHAT IS THE ADVANTAGE OF A SMART OBJECT?
1. It keeps the original resolution. Even if you make the layer smaller you can later make it bigger again.
2. It often keeps our files organized.

WHAT CAN'T YOU DO WITH A SMART OBJECT?
Anything pixel related. i.e. change eye color, remove a pimple, whiten teeth…

WHAT DO YOU DO IF YOU NEED TO MAKE PIXEL RELATED CHANGES?
Double click on the smart object icon on the layer (it looks like a file) and it will open another file- on this file you can pixel changes. Once you save it and exit, they will appear on your original file.

WHAT IS THE DIFFERENCE BETWEEN LINKED AND EMBEDDED?
LINKED- it can link it to a psd, png, tiff… and if you need a change, when you save it it will CHANGE your original file.

EMBEDDED- it makes a copy of the file in photoshop and it's saved hidden inside your file. If you change it, it will change in your file, but it won't change the original picture. (your photoshop file will be heavier)

HOW DO YOU CREATE A SMART OBJECT?
1. When you Place an image in photoshop, by using file>place by default it's a smart object.
2. If you already have a layer in photoshop that you would like to change it into a smart object. Right click on the layer and choose "convert to smart object"

WHAT IS THE OPPOSITE OF A SMART OBJECT?
PIXELS! rasterizing a layer changes it back to regular pixels.

quick review!
MASKING TROUBLESHOOTING

1. Make sure you are on your mask part of your layer

2. Make sure you are 100% black (000000) or 100% white (ffffff)

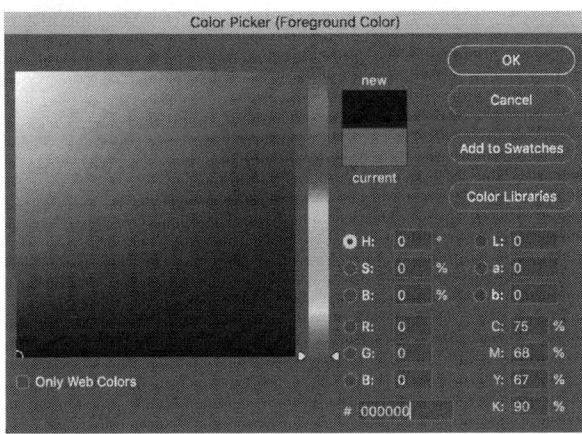

3. Make sure that the opacity and flow are at 100%

4. Make sure that you are on a "normal" brush

quick review!
LICE

1. Open your .eps file called more bugs, make sure to choose 300 dpi when you open the file.
2. Using your marquee tool, select the bug that looks most like a louse. make sure that your selection is not at all feathered. make sure that if you have a layer mask that you are selected on your layer part and not your mask part of your layer.
3. Go to edit>define brush preset and name your brush
4. Create a new layer
5. Choose your new brush from your options toolbar.
6. Then "toggle your brush panel" by clicking on the icon that looks like a cup with brushes, then you can play around with your options by clicking on the words. Jitter means change, so choose scattering and size jitter (they will then come in various sizes...)
7. Double click on your layer to give it a drop shadow.

quick review!
BOILS

CLONING PIMPLES:
1. Open an image of an egyptian and an image of a pimple
2. To use your clone tool from one file to another, they both need to be the same color mode (by the pimple you may need to go to image>mode>cmyk) then choose your clone stamp tool and click alt on the source (the pimple) make sure that on your options toolbar "aligned" is NOT checked off.
3. Go to the image with the Egyptian and create a new layer. Then with your clone stamp (already selected) you can paint the pimples.
4. Apply a blending mode like multiply to your layer with the pimples.

COPY AND MANIPULATE A BLISTER:
1. Open the image with the blister, select the blister and copy it. (control + C)
2. Go to your egyptian and paste the blister (control +V)
3. Transform and warp it
4. You can apply a blending mode
5. To blur it you first convert it for smart filters (filter>convert for smart filters) then you can give it a blur> gaussian blur to blur the edges
6. If that isn't good enough you can give the layer a mask and using a soft brush you can erase some of the edges

ANOTHER OPTION:
1. Bring the blister into the image of the egyptian
2. Select the blister and mask it
3. Feather the mask edges
4. Double click on your layer to give it a layer style. I chose an outer glow, the color a reddish pink, I used the darken color mode and made the size of it bigger.

quick review!
GRASSHOPPERS

1. Open your background (field)
2. File place your grasshopper (when you place it's automatically a smart object)
3. Mask it using color range
4. If there are white lines around it, erase them with masking now. (if you create a pattern they will be part of your pattern!)
5. Duplicate it 2x's to have 3 grasshoppers
6. Make them the size that you want your pattern to be
7. Turn the visibility off your background layer (the eye)
8. Use your marquee tool (make sure it's not feathered) to select create a marching ants around the grasshoppers
9. Make sure that you are not on the mask part of your layer
10. Go to Edit>define pattern
11. Go to your pattern stamp tool and on your option toolbar select the pattern that you just created.
12. Create a new layer and use your pattern stamp tool to paint on the grasshoppers

TO MAKE ANOTHER PATTERN WITH SMALLER OR BIGGER GRASSHOPPERS:
1. Select the original three grasshoppers, hold shift to select all 3
2. use your move tool to make them bigger or smaller (they are smart objects so it's ok)
3. Turn the visibility off your background layer (the eye)
4. Use your marquee tool (make sure it's not feathered) to select create a marching ants around the grasshoppers
5. Make sure that you are not on the mask part of your layer
6. Go to Edit>define pattern
7. Go to your pattern stamp tool and on your option toolbar select the pattern that you just created.
8. Create a new layer and use your pattern stamp tool to paint on the grasshoppers

TO CHANGE THEIR COLOR RANGE:
1. Use an adjustment layer (black and white cookie) on top of the layer that you want to apply the adjustment to.
2. Cick "alt" between the layers so that it only applies the adjustment mode to the layer under it.
3. Add a few big grasshoppers by duplicating and transforming the original layer.

quick review!
HAIL

1. Open your background (I chose a field on fire)
2. file>place and bring in your fire (I chose fire3.jpeg)
3. give your fire a mask, double click on the mask, choose color range. (make sure invert is checked) In color range select the black, you can bring the fuzziness up since it's ok if some of the fire becomes transparent. If need to delete more of the black or gray, choose the eyedropper tool with the plus sign and click on the color that you need deleted. Press ok.
4. file>place a picture of ice
5. select the ice using your quick selection tool and then click on your mask tool.
6. give a blending mode (pin light or hard light often work best)

IF YOU WANT SOME FIRE LEAPING OUT OF THE ICE:
1. Duplicate the layer of the fire
2. Bring it above the layer of the ice

Using your brush tool you mask away the part of the fire that you don't want in front of the ice.

TO MAKE THE FIRE AND ICE NOT EXACTLY THE SAME IN EACH ONE:
1. Duplicate the 3 layers of fire, ice and fire above.
2. Merge them
3. Filter> liquify and have fun :)

TO MAKE THE FIRE AND ICE NOT EXACTLY THE SAME IN EACH ONE:
1. Duplicate the 3 layers of fire, ice and fire above.
2. Merge them

IF YOU WANT SOME FIRE LEAPING OUT OF THE ICE:
1. Duplicate the 3 layers of fire, ice and fire above.
2. Merge them
3. Filter> liquify and have fun :)

TO CREATE A PATTERN::
1. Turn the visibility off your background layer (the eye)
2. Use your marquee tool (make sure it's not feathered) to select create a marching ants around the hail
3. Make sure that you are not on the mask part of your layer
4. Go to Edit>define pattern
5. Go to your pattern stamp tool and on your option toolbar select the pattern that you just created.
6. Create a new layer and use your pattern stamp tool to paint on the hail

IF YOU WANT THE PATTERN TO COME UP AS ITS OWN LAYER WITHOUT BRUSHING:
1. Click on the adjustment layer icon (b&w cookie) at the bottom of the layers panel
2. choose the pattern adjustment mode
3. Choose the size (do not make it larger than 100%, it will become pixelated)
4. You can use your mask tool if you want to erase any part of the pattern.

quick review! SHADOWS

BASIC SHADOW:
1. Duplicate your layer of your animal (it needs to be masked out already)
2. Go to Layer Styles (double click on empty area) add a color overlay of the shadow color (click on the WORDS color overlay) and you can choose your color from your image by using the eyedropper that appears.
3. Control + T, hold down control to distort it into the direction you need it to go (middle top square of bounding box and dragging down) press enter to apply
4. drag your layer behind/ under your animal layer
5. In your layers panel you can bring the opacity down
6. Double click on your mask to then feather it
7. If necessary use your black brush on your mask to get rid of any white lines that appear from masking

TO MAKE A SHADOW CLIMB A WALL:
1. After you create a shadow using the instructions above:
2. Duplicate your shadow layer
3. Turn the eye off of one of the shadows
4. Erase (with your masking tools) the shadow once it hits the wall
5. Turn the eye on your other shadow, erase the parts of the shadow before the wall
6. At this point you may want to rasterize your layer (right click, rasterize layer) and apply your mask to the pixels. (drag your mask into the garbage can, and when the warning appears choose apply)
7. Edit>transform>distort, to position your mask as you need it.

IF YOUR IMAGE COMES WITH A GOOD SHADOW AND IT'S ON A WHITE BACKGROUND:
1. Duplicate your layer
2. Isolate just your object and mask it
3. Select your layer without the mask and give it a "multiply" blending mode (on your layers panel to the left of opacity- it usually saids normal)
4. Put the layer with your blending mode behind your layer with the mask

quick review!
MAKE A FUN POSTCARD

TO SET UP YOUR DOC:
File>Document Setup:
put in the measurements of the card
CardsinthePost.com: (uk) 151mm x 106mm
Postcardsanywhere.com: (usa) 6x4.25in

TO PLACE YOUR BACKGROUND:
1. Click on your Rectangle placeholder tool to create the frame for your background image. You click drag and release once it's the size you want it to be.
2. File> place and choose the folder of "Papers" to choose a nice background

Right click on the frame and choose>fitting>fit frame proportionally

TO BRING IN AN IMAGE:
1. You can press control+D to bring in your image and then click and drag to create your frame the size you would like
2. or, you can create the frame first like you did for your background.
3. Repeat this for any elements that you would like on your card (flowers...)

TO ADD TEXT:
1. Click on your Type tool "T"
2. Create a text frame, You click drag and release once it's the size you want it to be.
3. Type your message, you could choose your font and size on your options toolbar
4. To choose a color for your text select your text (not your frame) and double click on the color picker at the bottom of your toolbox.

TO ADD A STROKE:
To choose a color for your text select your text (not your frame) and double click on the color picker at the bottom of your toolbox. (make sure you are selected on the stroke and not the fill)

TIPS:
- Control + Shift allows you to transform your object and content together.
- To select an object below to object that you are clicked on you hold down control and click
- Right click and choose arrange>bring to front or back to rearrange the order of your object
- For your fitting options right click on your object and choose fitting>... your most commonly used option is "fill frame proportionally"

this works well for photos on a solid background

MASKING USING COLOR RANGE

1. Click on the layer you want to Mask
2. Add a layer mask by clicking on your mask icon at the bottom of your layers panel (square with circle inside it)
3. Double click on the mask part of your layer to bring up your "mask properties" panel
4. Choose color range
5. Click where you can guess your background is
6. Check off inverse at the right hand of your panel
7. If your background has more than one color, choose the eyedropper with a + sign to hide more colors

TIPS:
- Use your fuzziness to choose how much of the color it should take, when working with your animals you're usually better off taking more of the background off and giving the animal a fur cut :)
- If any area inside the animal got deleted that you don't want to: Hold down "Alt" and click on the mask part of your layer and brush using your white layer.
- Go to your masking properties and click on "mask edge" to adjust and perfect the edges.

MASKING TRICKS
TO MAKE AN OBJECT APPEAR BEHIND ANOTHER OBJECT

To make the girrafe go behind the pillar

1. Duplicate the background layer by right clicking on the background layer and choosing "duplicate layer"

2. Drag the background copy above all the layers (all I see now is my background)
3. Use a selection tool to select pillar
4. Click on the masking icon at the bottom of your layers panel to create a mask.

All done!

quick review
MAKE SCATTERED STARS WITH YOUR BRUSH TOOL

1. Choose your brush tool
2. Create a new layer
3. Click on your brush shape on your option tool bar
4. Choose your gear icon
5. Choose to load your assorted brushes
6. Choose your star brush
7. Click on the icon that looks like a cup with brushes in it
8. In the brush panel, choose your options, scattering, color dynamics... Jitter means that there will be changes some bigger and some smaller.... in your brush panel don't just select, click on the words to control your options

clipping mask in photoshop
CREATE A PHOTO IN A FLOWER SHAPE IN PS

1. Choose custom shapes
2. On your option toolbar you can choose to reset your shapes to "nature" (by clicking on the shape and then on the gear icon)
3. Choose a flower
4. draw a flower
5. file> place an image
6. press enter
7. the image needs to be on top of your shape
8. click "alt" between the layers to clip the photo into the shape
9. link the layers at the bottom of your link panel so they move together

SETTING A BOOK COVER
WITH A SPINE IN INDESIGN

1. Set up your file with the page size of your front and back cover

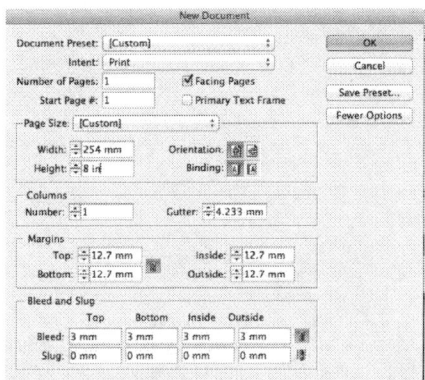

2. Go to the bottom of the pages panel and click on the icon that allows you to edit the page size

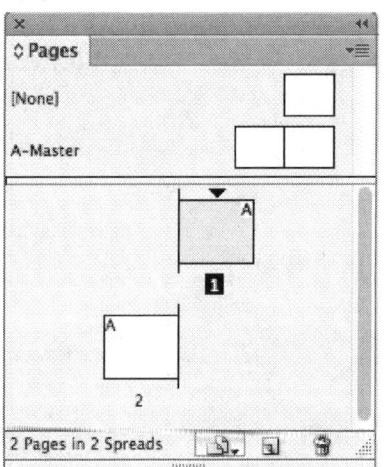

3. Choose custom size, type in the name "spine" put in the sizes, landscape.click on add and then click "ok"

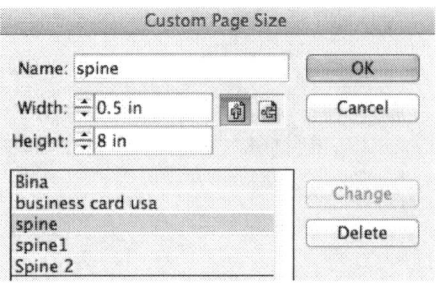

4. If you get a margins warning, go to the menu on the top, choose "layout"> margins and columns. Change it to 3mm or .125 in

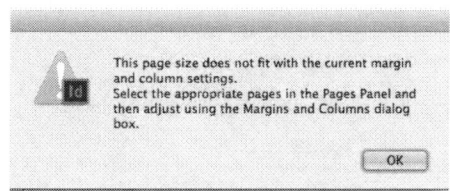

5. Add a page and select page 2

6: Click on your "edit page size" and choose the preset that you just created

7: Right click on your pages panel and unclick "allow document pages to shuffle"

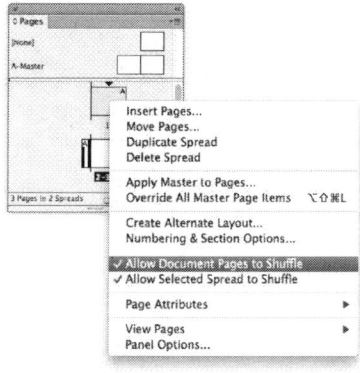

8: Drag page one near page 2, and you are done!

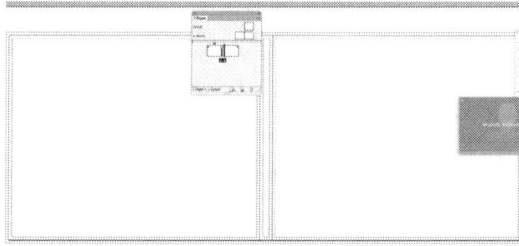

Make sure to check for errors before making your pdf

CUSTOMIZING A PREFLIGHT PROFILE

1. To create a custom preflight profile, open the Preflight dialog (Window > Output > Preflight), and choose Define Profiles from the flyout menu.

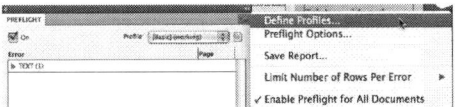

2. In the Preflight Profiles dialog, you first want to add a profile. You can't edit the [Basic] profile. Click on the + button. Give it a name (I named mine "Production"), and click Save.

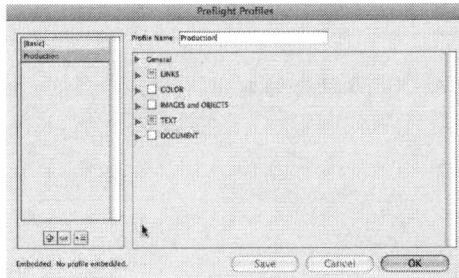

3. Next, you want to choose the attributes you want to check for in the profile. It will require some experience and experimentation to decide what criteria to include.

For most environments, you probably want to define different profiles for the different kinds of output you do regularly. It might be tempting to make a profile with every possible option checked, but that will end up being more trouble than it's worth. In the example below, I've added the ability to look for low resolution images by checking the options under Image Resolution.

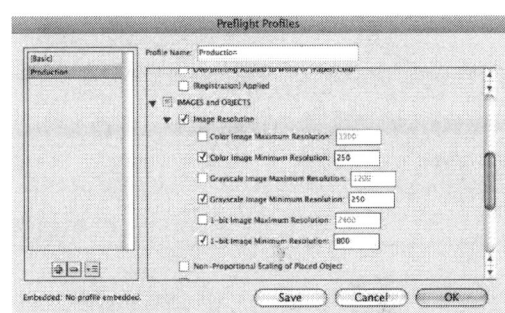

4. After making your choices, click OK. Now, for the customized preflight profile to be active, you must select it from the list of profiles. When you do, InDesign will immediately analyze the InDesign file using the new profile.

PREFLIGHT

Before sending a document off to print, do a preflight to check for any errors.

Common errors that come up are, missing fonts, overset text, image resolution.

What to do if you are missing a font;
1) You can sync the font from your adobe typekit
2) Buy or download the font and install on your system
3) You may decide to change your font and replace

Step 1 go to file package
On left hand side press font
Check off show problems only

Choose find font
Again select font you want changed
At bottom of panel you can choose which font you want to replace with

You can select replace all
Advisable to press redefine style

What to do if you have overset text;
Click on the page number it will take you to the page with the error.
Either enlarge the text box or make the text size smaller.

For a preflight checking for low resolution;
Click 'define profiles' at the bottom of your screen
Create new, name it check resolution.
Don't check off too much.
Go to images and objects and check off
Non-proportional scaling of placed objects
Image resolution (colour minimum of 250 is fine)
Press save

Now change preflight profile from basic to check resolution.

CREATE A PRESS QUALITY PDF

1. There are many different ways to convert an Indesign document to PDF. We are covering one way. Before you send your document to the printer speak to them to know how they want th file prepared.

2. From InDesign, choose File > Export and select Adobe PDF in the format field.

3. In the Export To PDF dialog box, select High Quality Print, or Press Quality (if it is for a press offset printer) as the Adobe PDF Preset.

   If the file has a bleed and needs crop marks, enter that information by "Marks and Bleeds"

   Finish by clicking EXPORT.

NOTE:
There are plenty of more options these are the very basic instructions.

- If you are emailing it and need it in low resolution, choose "smallest document size"
- If you want only a range of pages, select that in the first panel.
- If you need it as spreads click that on the first panel.

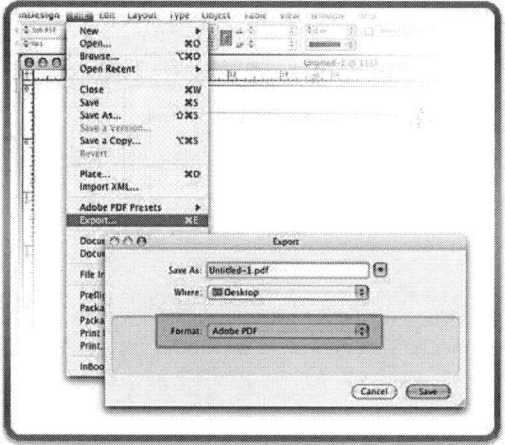

UNIT TWO
BRANDING

If there is one thing that we can learn from famous logos like Nike's "Swoosh" or FedEx logo, it is that the logo does not have to be complicated to be effective.
Hopefully, this collection of famous logo designs will help prove that simplicity and color is the key to a memorable logo.

The famous Coca-Cola logo was created by John Pemberton's bookkeeper, Frank Mason Robinson, in 1885.

Pepsi-Cola logo has changed many times over the years. The logo that is used right now was introduced in 2009.

The Audi emblem is four overlapping rings that represent the four marques of Auto Union. The Audi emblem symbolizes Audi amalgamation of Audi with DKW, Horch and Wanderer: the first ring represents Audi, the second represents DKW, third is Horch, and the fourth and last ring Wanderer.

The Apple logo was created in 1976 by Rob Janoff. The rainbow color theme was used until 1998.

Chanel logo is an overlapping double 'C' - one facing forward and the other facing backward.

The company registered as adidas AG (with lower-case lettering) on 18 August 1949. The company's clothing and shoe designs typically feature three parallel stripes, and this same motif is incorporated into Adidas's current official logo.

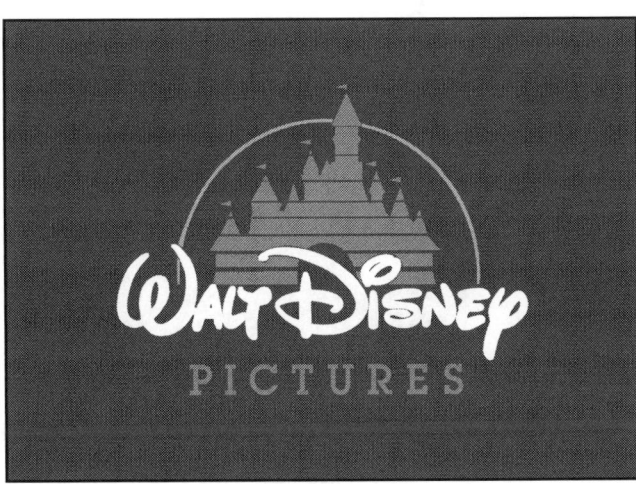

The Walt Disney logo is a 'stylized version of the founder's signature' that signifies the brand name and promises secure, cheerful and quality American mainstream entertainment.

The FedEx logo is notable for containing a hidden right-pointing arrow in the negative space between the "E" and the "X".

The McDonald's Golden Arches logo was introduced in 1962. It was created by Jim Schindler to resemble new arch shaped signs on the sides of the restaurants. He merged the two golden arches together to form the famous 'M' now recognized throughout the world.

Logomark

Logotype

Define your brand

What do you want people to think about when they see your client's new logo, direct mail piece, web site or advertisement? When customers think of strong brands, they usually think of short phrases or single words. The stronger and clearer the brand, usually the more focused the message (brand) is in the minds of consumers. Here are strong brands and the words people associate with them:

- Harley-Davidson - rebellion and freedom on the open road
- FedEx - overnight shipping
- Taco Bell - Mexican fast food
- Nike - high-performance athletic shoes
- Subway - eat fresh, and freshly made sub sandwiches
- Tide - clean clothes
- X-games - extreme sports games
- Krispy Kreme donuts - tasty glazed donuts
- Starbucks - gourmet, high-end coffee
- Coke - cola (especially in the South)
- Mercedes - luxury car
- Porsche - luxury sports car
- Red Bull - energy drink
- Timex - value-priced, durable watches
- Hersheys - chocolate candy bar

Hidden Messages in logos

IDENTITY DESIGN

Technical skill is mastery of complexity, while creativity is mastery of simplicity.
– Christopher Zeeman

- The design brief
- Brainstorming
- Researching
- Sketching
- Rendering / prototype
- Creative presentation / Client feedback
- Finishing touches / Revisions
- File creation and supply

Adapted from: Logo Design Love by David Airey

The Design Brief

When you're dealing with a graphic or logo design project, it's vital to write a detailed design brief at the very beginning. There are two main reasons for this:

- Firstly, it ensures that you, as a business owner or in-house manager know exactly what you want to achieve from your project.

- Second, the brief acts as a point of reference for designers, giving them key points to focus on.

SAMPLE CLIENT QUESTIONS:
Please tell me about your business.
What type of products or services do you offer?
Who is your target audience?
Who are your competitors?
What are your preferred colors?
What is your design style?
What type of fonts do you like?
What type of designs do you like? (please show 3 logos)
Any additional information that I may find useful?

This means less time — therefore less money — is spent on the result. The crux of the matter is this: The more information you provide at the beginning of the project, the more value for money you'll receive from your graphic / logo designer.

To help get you started, I've set out some pointers when writing your graphic design brief. Consider including your:

CORPORATE PROFILE
Don't assume that people know you well. Incorrect assumptions about you can render the entire opening discussion absolutely meaningless. Provide a summary of your business along with a brief history.

MARKET POSITION
A realistic evaluation of your company, service, or brand relative to your what the competition is doing.

CURRENT SITUATION
Explain what's happening to bring about the need for this project. For instance, a new product launch that needs advertising.

COMMUNICATION BACKGROUND
This includes both previous and present communication activity, such as research, advertising, direct mail, graphic design, public relations etc.

COMMUNICATION TASK — "THE MESSAGE"
What's the context of the specific message in relation to your business plans?
Include pieces of information to be shown in the designed item e.g. text, logos, images etc.

TARGET MARKET
Demographics — the age, gender, income, employment, geography, lifestyle of those you want to reach.

OBJECTIVES
What do you want to achieve? Make your objectives specific and the results measurable.

SCHEDULE AND DEADLINE
Give your designer a detailed and realistic schedule of how you would like the project to advance. Take the following into consideration:

- Consultation (research, strategy, brief development)
- Creative (concept and design development)
- Production (artwork, printing and other production)
- Delivery

If, as a designer, you're dealing with a client who hasn't produced a design brief, it's important to have your own template that you can send them at the beginning. This shows the client your professionalism and ultimately saves them time and money.

MIND MAPPING

Tony Buzan is widely credited with coining the term mind map. Mind maps are a means of organizing information visually, showing how big ideas are made of big pieces, which in turn are composed of smaller pieces. The famous inventor and artist Leonardo daVinci created diagrams similar to mind maps hundreds of years ago as a means of organizing information.

Buzan has defined ten guidelines for effective mind mapping, which we're reviewing for your benefit.

1. Start in the center with an image of the topic, using at least 3 colors. The center is the key because, as you will see, the ideas documented in a mind map radiate from the center of diagram, similar the branches or root system of a tree. The colors are important because they provide an extra dimension of information to help your brain interpret the data more effectively.

2. Use images, symbols, codes, and dimensions throughout your Mind Map. Words are important, but pictures make it easier and faster to communicate information visually. Similarly, symbols, codes and dimensions provide a mental shorthand to speed up the communication process. Of course, these different symbols, code and dimensions should be simple enough that a wide variety of people can easily interpret what's in the mind map.

3. Select key words and print using upper or lower case letters. Key words work well with images to convey information, similar to the way slides work in presentations. Printing makes them legible.

4. Each word/image is best alone and sitting on its own line. This is to make the mind map easy to interpret. Too many uncoordinated lines makes for a confusing mind map. The lines should be connected, starting from the central image. The central lines are thicker, organic and flowing, becoming thinner as they radiate out from the centre.

5. The idea here is to give the reader a visual guide as to the level of detail they're at within a mind map. Obviously, if you follow the lines through the map, you'll see how everything is connected. Varying thicknesses will make the mind map look like a system of branches or roots. Make the lines the same length as the word/image they support. Again, readability is the key

6. Use multiple colors throughout the Mind Map, for visual stimulation and also to encode or group.

7. Much like bus routes and subway maps use color to distinguish between routes, use of color in a mind map will make it easier to follow the information.

8. Develop your own personal style of Mind Mapping. Personal style allows you to create mind maps more efficiently and effectively.

9. Use emphasis and show associations in your Mind Map. This allows you to focus attention on key topics in the mind map.

10. Keep the Mind Map clear by using radial hierarchy, numerical order or outlines to embrace your branches. What do these things mean? Numerical order and outlines are pretty straight forward, but what is radial hierarchy? Put simply, radial hierarchy is information organized by most important information in the center and more detailed information situated farther and farther away from the diagram's center.

BRAINSTORMING

> You cannot use up creativity. The more you use the more you have.
> – Maya Angelou

FIND YOUR FAVORITE "CREATIVE" ENVIRONMENT and complete brainstorming wheel one on your own. Imagine yourself transported into your client's "brand experience." This could be their retail store, web site, packaging, product, etc. What do you see?… feel?… hear?… etc. Write down at least 10 ideas per category. This may take some time. You do not have to do it all at once. Sometimes, small breaks (of 1 hour to 1 day) helps to separate yourself from the problem and start thinking with a fresh mind again.

THE GOAL OF BRAINSTORMING IS TO GET YOUR MIND thinking of all the different creative directions and elements you could use to communicate your client's brand and message to the target market. Don't limit yourself when you brainstorm. Get crazy and free with your ideas. It will help you break free from the "tired" old ideas that we have all seen too often.

REMEMBER, CREATIVITY DOESN'T ALWAYS FLOW FREELY, it needs nurturing and nourishment. If you're not feeling creative in one environment, change it and move to a different room, or go outside, or to a coffee shop or restaurant, etc. You may also try taking a walk outside to help clear your mind and get the creative juices flowing again. Some people take a snack break to refuel and then get back to work. Chocolate works wonders!

RESEARCH

I spend time reviewing client information and begin the research and brainstorming stage. Here I take into account client competition, trends in the market, what sets the client apart, the history of the business, the future, the current brand, and the one aspired toward.

In order to create original design work for your clients, you must first educate yourself on the client's industry and competition. You cannot create something new unless you know what everyone else is doing. During your research you will also come across design and marketing strategies and trends that will keep you (and your client's projects) fresh, appropriate and up-to-date. You do not want to create something that you think is original only to find out that it looks just like your client's competition. Your client will not be impressed.

It is therefore very important to research the industry, and understand the general graphic design style. We are not designing on a blank canvas.

SOME GOOD WEBSITES FOR LOGO INSPIRATION:

Logopond
Creattica
LogoFury
LogoLog
Logo Design Love
LOGOFI
Logo Moose
Logo Faves
LogoGala
The Design inspiration
Logo Sause
Logo Of The Day
Logolicia
Stationary Style
Logospire
Logo Lounge
Logoed
Logogallery
Logo Galleria
Logorium

DESIGNING A LOGO

A good logo design should be able to be drawn in sand with a piece of stick.

What is Logo Design?

Advantages of logo design:
-
-
-
-

What to look for in a logo design?
-
-
-
-

What to avoid in logo design?
-
-
-
-

ILLUSTRATOR TOOLBOX

The toolbox contains the main tools for designing. Click any tool to select and use it.

A small arrow next to a tool in the toolbox indicates that the tool also has additional options available. In Photoshop, click and hold your mouse on a tool to see its options. For example, if you click and hold on the select tool, you'll see select options such as eliptical selction, single row selection, etc.

Tool Options
When you select a tool, additional options appear in the Tool Options bar (by default this is located just below the main menu).

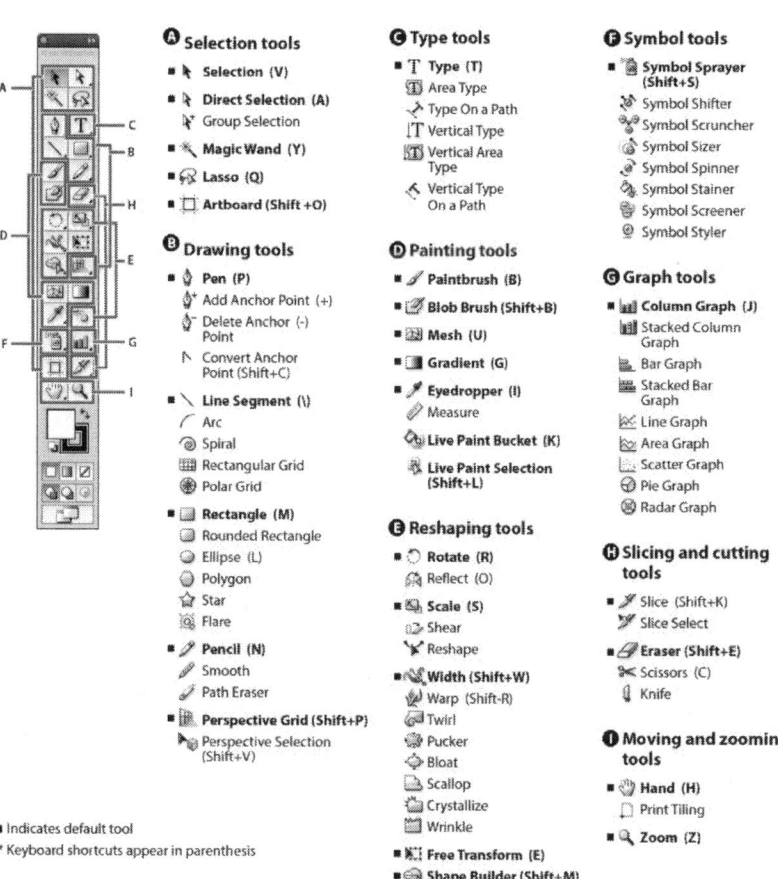

"We can't solve problems by using the same kind of thinking we used when we created them."

—Albert Einstein

selection tools
ILLUSTRATOR TOOLBOX

Tool: _____

Function: _____

Tool: _____

Function: _____

Tool: _____

Function: _____

Tool: _____

Function: _____

Tool: _____

Function: _____

Tool: _____

Function: _____

> You can't do better design with a computer, but you can speed up your work enormously.
>
> — Wim Crouwel

drawing tools
ILLUSTRATOR TOOLBOX

Tool: _____

Function:

Tool: _____

Function:

Tool: _____

Function:

Tool: _____

Function:

Tool: _____

Function:

Tool: _____

Function:

Tool: _____

Function:

Tool: _____

Function:

drawing tools
ILLUSTRATOR TOOLBOX

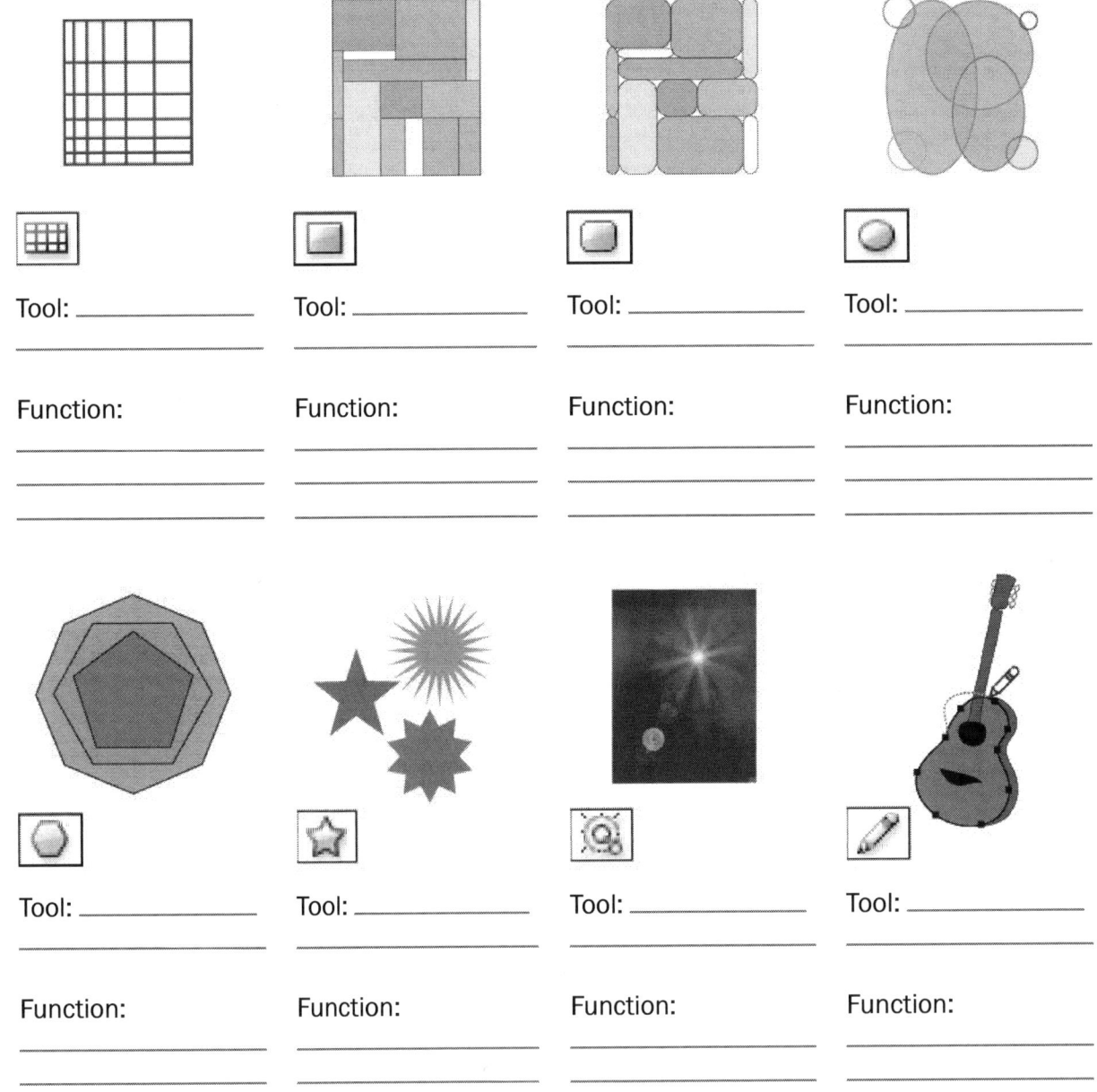

Tool: _____

Function: _____

Tool: _____

Function: _____

Tool: _____

Function: _____

Tool: _____

Function: _____

Tool: _____

Function: _____

Tool: _____

Function: _____

Tool: _____

Function: _____

Tool: _____

Function: _____

drawing tools
ILLUSTRATOR TOOLBOX

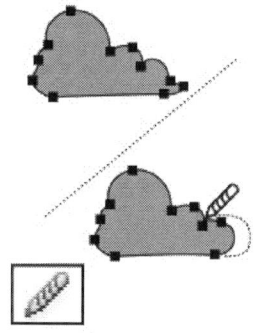

Tool: _____

Function: _____
_____

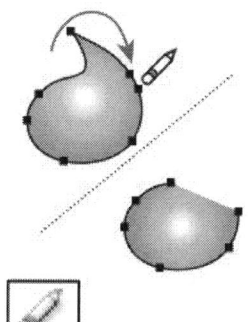

Tool: _____

Function: _____
_____

Tool: _____

Function: _____
_____

Tool: _____

Function: _____
_____

type tools
ILLUSTRATOR TOOLBOX

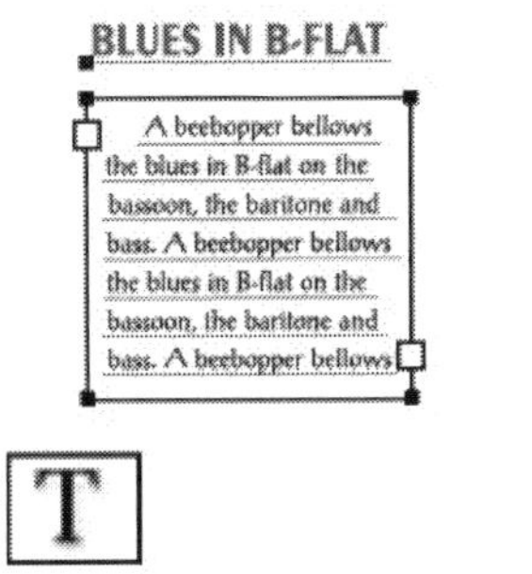

Tool: _____

Function:

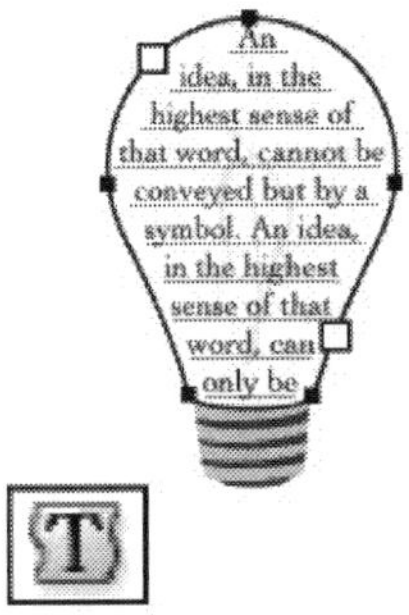

Tool: _____

Function:

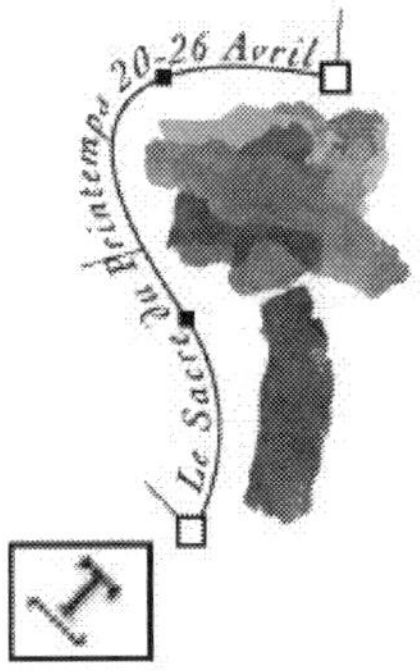

Tool: _____

Function:

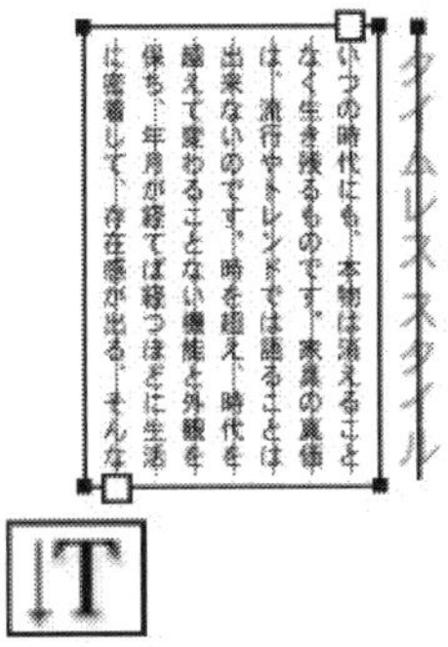

Tool: _____

Function:

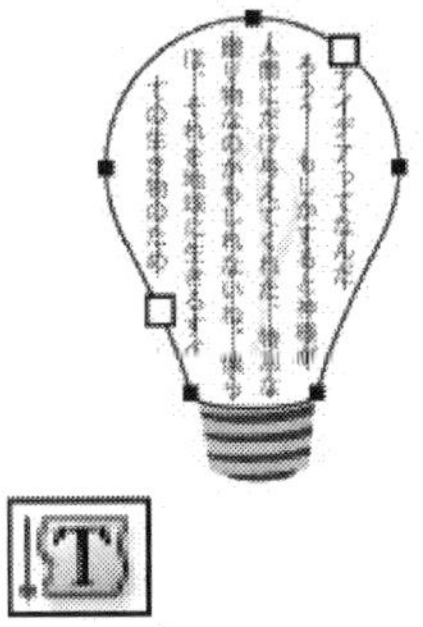

Tool: _____

Function:

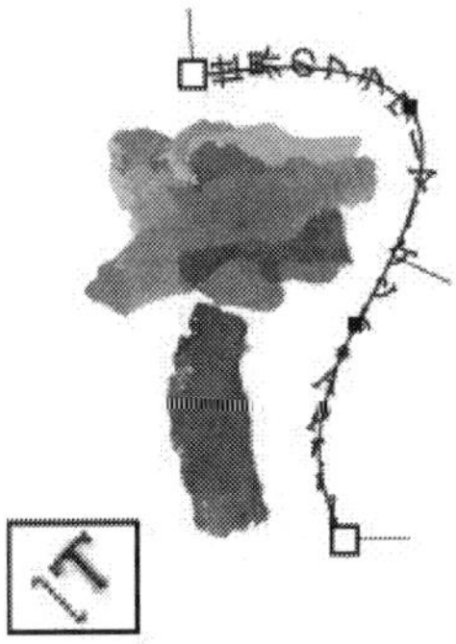

Tool: _____

Function:

Technology over technique produces emotionless design.

— Daniel Mall

painting tools
ILLUSTRATOR TOOLBOX

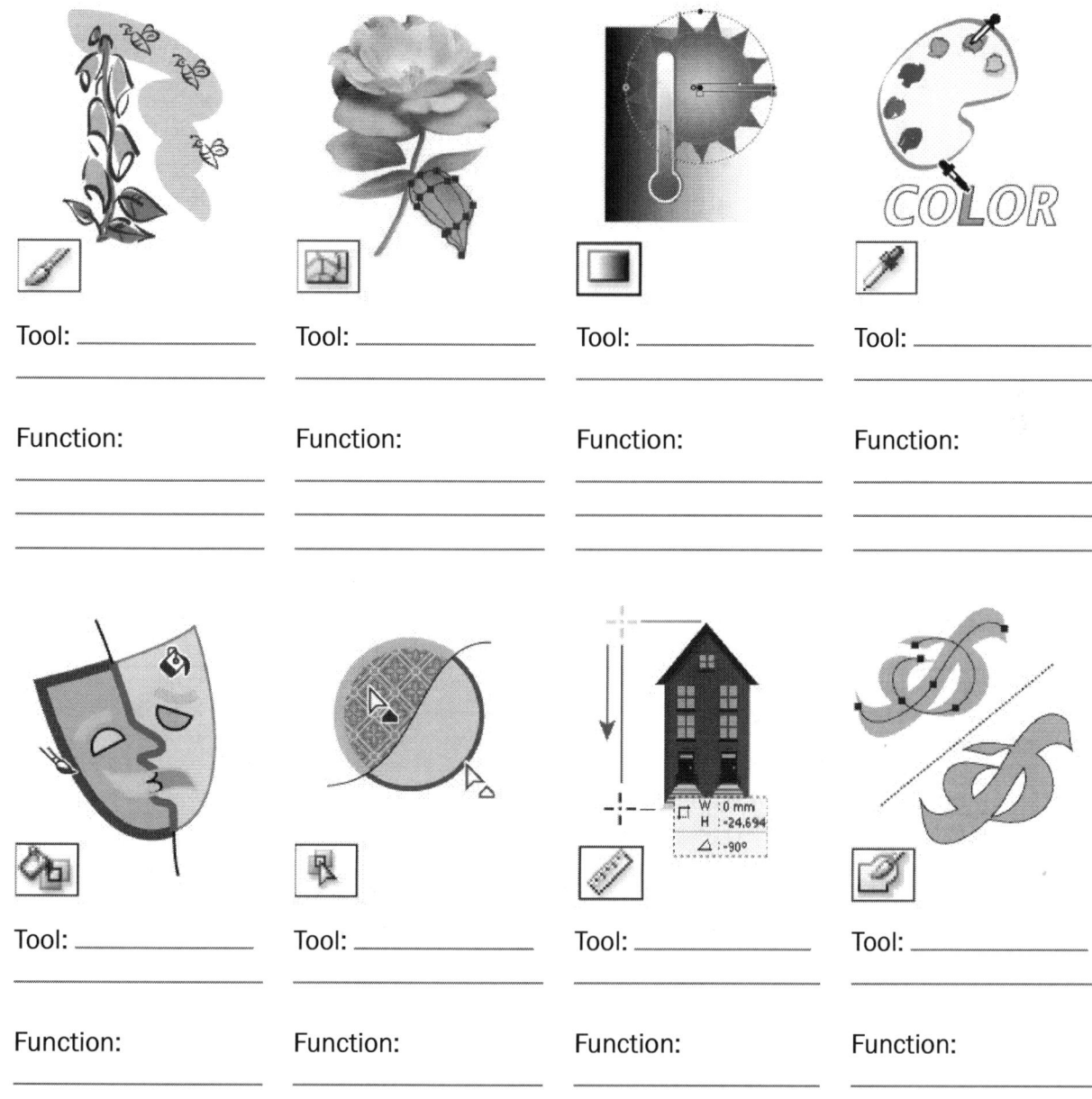

Tool: _____

Function:

Tool: _____

Function:

Tool: _____

Function:

Tool: _____

Function:

Tool: _____

Function:

Tool: _____

Function:

Tool: _____

Function:

Tool: _____

Function:

reshaping tools
ILLUSTRATOR TOOLBOX

Tool: _____

Function: _____

Tool: _____

Function: _____

Tool: _____

Function: _____

Tool: _____

Function: _____

Tool: _____

Function: _____

Tool: _____

Function: _____

Tool: _____

Function: _____

Tool: _____

Function: _____

reshaping tools
ILLUSTRATOR TOOLBOX

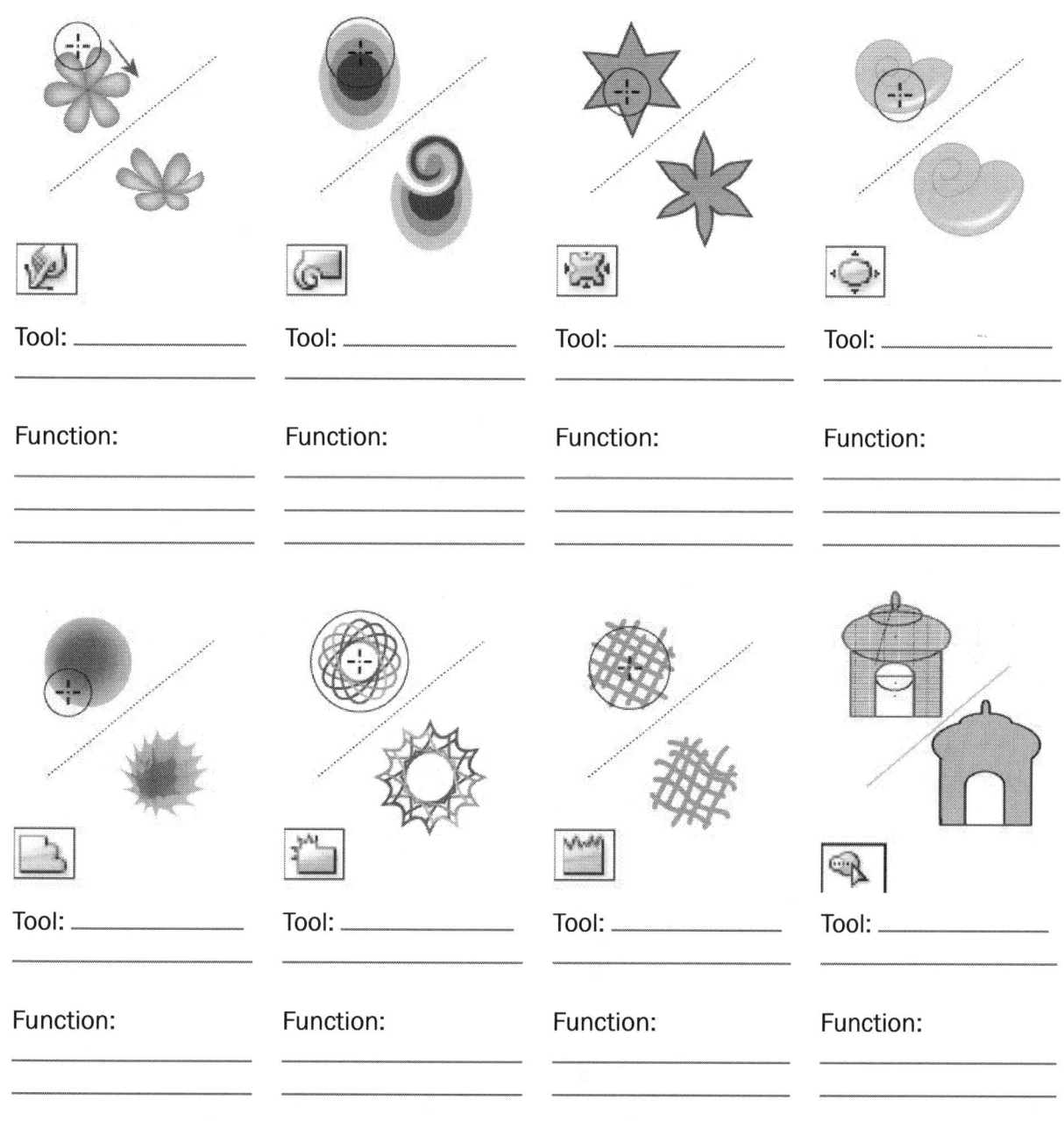

Tool: _____

Function:

Tool: _____

Function:

Tool: _____

Function:

Tool: _____

Function:

Tool: _____

Function:

Tool: _____

Function:

Tool: _____

Function:

Tool: _____

Function:

symbolism tools
ILLUSTRATOR TOOLBOX

The symbolism tools let you create and modify sets of symbol instances. You create a symbol set using the Symbol Sprayer tool. You can then use the other symbolism tools to change the density, color, location, size, rotation, transparency, and style of the instances in the set.

Tool: _____

Function: _____

Tool: _____

Function: _____

Tool: _____

Function: _____

Tool: _____

Function: _____

Tool: _____

Function: _____

Tool: _____

Function: _____

Tool: _____

Function: _____

Tool: _____

Function: _____

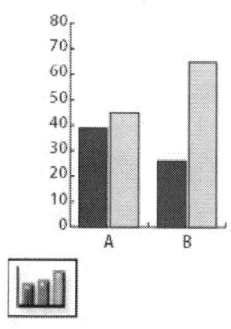

Tool: _____

Function: _____

graph tools
ILLUSTRATOR TOOLBOX

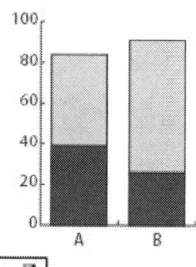 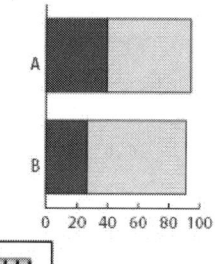 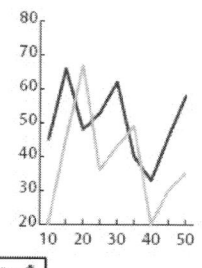

Tool: _____   Tool: _____   Tool: _____   Tool: _____

Function: Function: Function: Function:

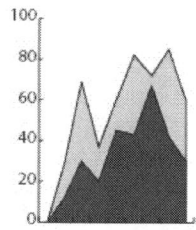 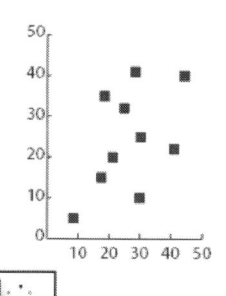 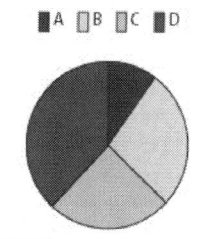 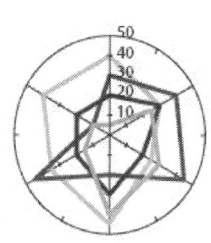

Tool: _____   Tool: _____   Tool: _____   Tool: _____

Function: Function: Function: Function:

slicing & cutting tools
ILLUSTRATOR TOOLBOX

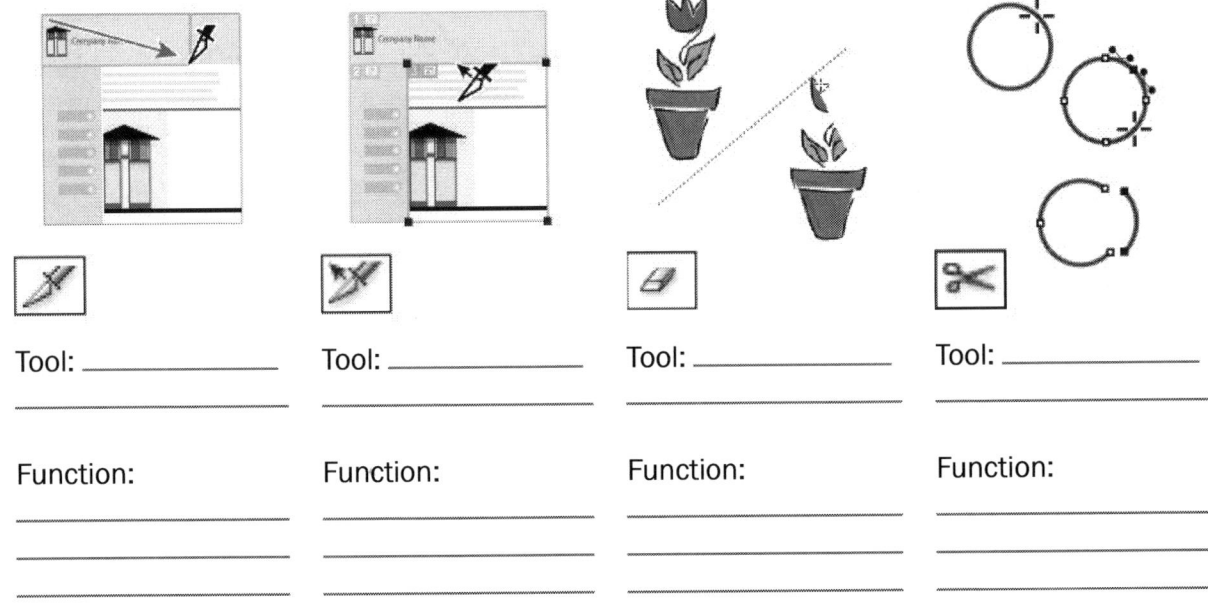

Tool: _____

Function:

Tool: _____

Function:

Tool: _____

Function:

Tool: _____

Function:

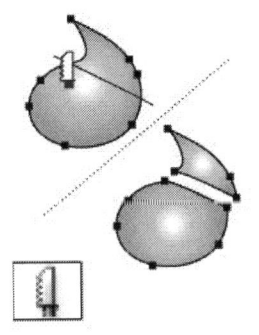

Tool: _____

Function:

Computers are to design as microwaves are to cooking.

— Milton Glaser

CREATE A BOARD LOGO

INSTRUCTIONS

1. Create a new document, in CMYK color mode. Size is not an issue, as you will be handing off the Illustrator file to the design team working on the album artwork. Name the project Comin At Ya.

2. Type the text Comin' At Ya. Use Point type, not Area type. (That is, click with the Type tool to create point type rather than click and drag to create area type.) Apply the Verdana font. Resize the type so it is pretty big size rangeing from 72 points to 150 point. Apply a bright-colored fill (not black) and no stroke.

3. With the text block selected, choose Effect > 3D > Extrude & Bevel to open the 3D Extrude & Bevel Options dialog box. Click Preview so you can see your changes as you make them.

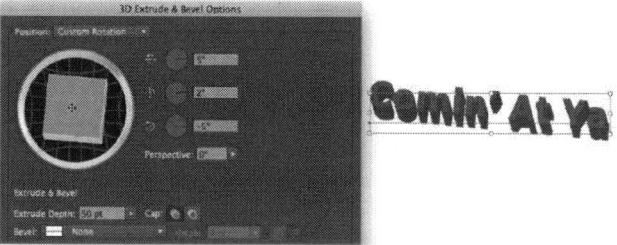

4. Experiment with the extrusion angle by manually manipulating the cube while observing the effect in the document.

5. Experiment with different Extrude & Bevel settings.

6. Click More Options in the 3D Extrude and Bevel Options dialog box. Experiment with different light source settings. Save the file as an Illustrator file with default .ai file settings.

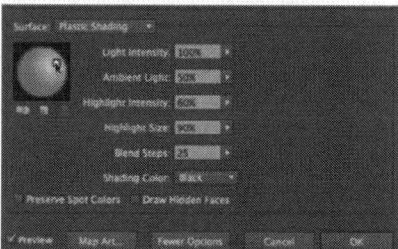

7. To tweak the design, add a warp effect (Object > Envelope Distort > Make With Warp).

8. As a final touchup, expand the warp (Object > Envelope Distort > Expand) and touch up the colors. Save the file as CominAtYa.ai, with Illustrator defaults.

DRESS CATALOG COLORING

INSTRUCTIONS

1. Open the file dress.ai or create a new file of your own with letter-size print defaults and with the CMYK color mode selected in the New Document dialog box.

2. Copy and paste the dress design to create two rows of three copies of the dress (six dresses in all).

3. Use the Direct Selection tool and the Color panel to apply the following colors to the three dresses in the first row (values represent percentages):

   - Dress 1 — main color: C=17, M=0, Y=51, K=0; highlight color: C=54, M=0, Y=32, K=0.

   - Dress 2 — main color: C=66, M=29, Y=91, K=0; highlight color: C=17, M=0, Y=51, K=0.

   - Dress 3 — main color: C=54, M=0, Y=32, K=0; highlight color: C=66, M=29, Y=91, K=0.

4. The dresses in the second row use colors from the Pantone color swatchbook (display that Swatches panel by choosing Window > Swatch Libraries > Color Books and selecting the Pantone+ Solid Coated set). Add the following Pantone colors from that book to your Swatches panel: 516C, 401C, and 5135C.

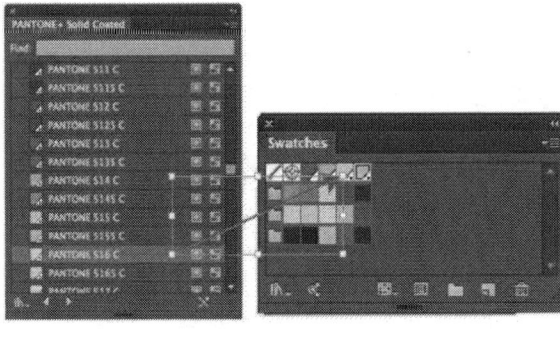

Still using the Direct Selection tool, apply the three Pantone colors (you decide how) to the dresses in the third row.

5. Save the file as an Illustrator (.ai) file with default settings. Name it Dress.ai

CREATE DRESS PATTERNS

INSTRUCTIONS

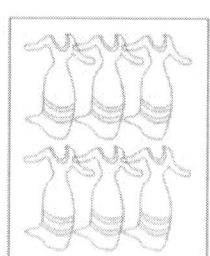

1. Open the file dress.ai or create a new file of your own with letter-size print defaults and with CMYK color mode selected in the New Document dialog box.

2. Copy and paste the dress design to create one, two, or three rows of three copies of the dress — your pick, depending on how much fun you want to have (more dresses = more fun).

3. Choose a pattern swatch library from which to select pattern fills for the dresses. If you wish, try the Decorative Legacy.

4. Select different sections of the dresses and apply patterns from your selected swatch library.

5. In the Scale tool dialog box, select Transform Patterns, and deselect Scale Strokes & Effects and Transform Objects. Experiment with different scaling values to modify the patterns (try both Uniform and Non-Uniform). Use the Preview check box to see the effect of scaling the pattern

   before you apply the new values by clicking OK.

6. Experiment with different swatches. When your set of designs is complete, save the file in Adobe Illustrator (.ai) format with default settings. Name the file Dress.ai

WORKING WITH BRUSHES

INSTRUCTIONS

1. Create a CMYK document — any size. Save it as lightning-yourname.ai.

2. Create the object that you want to use to create a custom art brush — in this case, a ribbon. From the Brush panel select the Artistic library. From the submenu select Artistic Calligraphic. Choose one of the Calligraphic brushes. Select the object and drag it to the Brush panel. Save it as an Art brush. Name it Ribbon. Experiment with color and shape to achieve the desired design.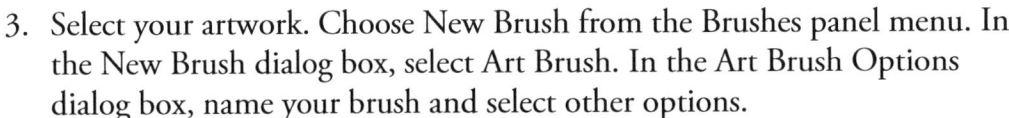

3. Select your artwork. Choose New Brush from the Brushes panel menu. In the New Brush dialog box, select Art Brush. In the Art Brush Options dialog box, name your brush and select other options.

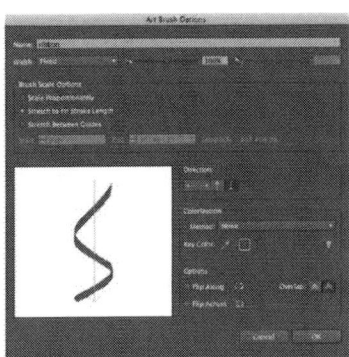

4. Create some alternate designs using one or more objects, and use design to create an art brush. Then draw a line or create an object with any of the object-creation tools (for example, the Rectangle tool), and apply your art brush to it.

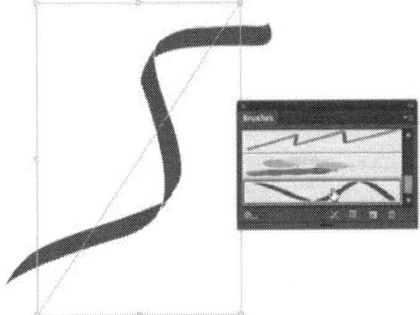

5. Save your project.

CREATING ART WITH LIVE PAINT

1. Open one of the live image files that was sent to you

2. Using www.color.adobe.com, create a theme scheme using triadic colors.
3. Click "control A" to select the image, color it in with your color theme.

Good luck.

CREATING A HOUSE FROM SHAPES

1. Open a page size w: 40/h:20 , and name it "exercise 1"
2. Save your page
3. Create each object on a separate layer, and give every layer a name in a group
4. You can use the white arrow- Direct selection tool, in order to change an object's points
5. Keep on saving your document.

Good luck.

CREATING ANIMALS AND REFLECTING THEM

1. Open a page size w: 29/h: 21 cm , and name it Reflecting animals
2. Save your page
3. Create background by creating a rectangle .
4. Draw a 3 rectangles in the middle of the page
5. With the shape tool create animals using the pathfinder and by using the method of drew in.
6. Select the animals and group then in to 1 group.
7. Duplicate the animal group and flip them over with flip horizontal.
8. Give the duplicate group an opacity of 40%
9. Create the tape with rectangles and stars and using the pathfinder

Good luck! .

CREATING FRUITS WITH PATHFINDER + SHAPEBUILDER

1. Open a Open a page size w: 20/h:15 cm and name it Creating fruits with pathfinder
2. Save your page
3. Create the fruit using pathfinder tool (window>pathfinder)

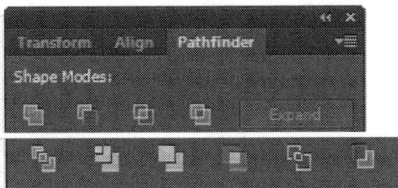

experiment with all of your pathfinder options that we discussed in class.

4. To combine shapes visually the shapebuilder tool is very useful. First select the shapes you want to combine, to add you drag your mouse over it and to substract you hold down "alt"

TRACE A PHOTO OF A FAMOUS BRIDGE

INSTRUCTIONS

1. Create a new document, in CMYK color mode. Size is not an issue, as you will be handing off the Illustrator file to a design team working on the book cover artwork. Name the project Bridge.

2. Place the photo bridge.jpg as an embedded (not linked) file.

3. Select the image. Select the Scale tool to scale the image to fit the artboard.

4. Choose View > Hide Artboards to remove any distraction. From the Image Trace preset pop-up menu, choose Black and White Logo.

5. Expand the trace by choosing Object > Image Trace > Expand.

6. Experiment with different Illustrator effects. Suggestion: try applying a slight warp (Object > Envelope Distort > Make With Warp).

7. Experiment with a Photoshop effect. Suggestion: try the Chalk & Charcoal effect (Effect > Sketch > Chalk & Charcoal).

8. Touch up the illustration by adding some surreal coloring. Save the file as Bridge.ai, with Illustrator default settings.

CREATE A FLOWER SHOW LOGO

INSTRUCTIONS

1. Open the file tulip.ai, or create a new file of your own with letter-sized print defaults and with CMYK Color Mode selected. If you open tulip.ai, use the Selection tool to familiarize yourself with the objects that make up the tulip.

2. Select one of the tulip-petal objects, and choose Object > Create Gradient Mesh. In the Create Gradient Mesh dialog box, define an 8-row-by-8-column flat mesh, with 50% highlighting.

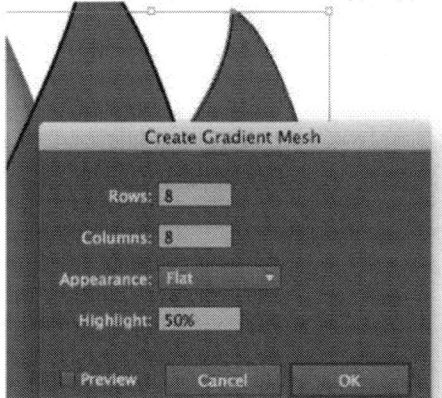

3. Use the Direct Selection tool to select individual anchor points within the gradient mesh. With the Direct Selection tool and the Color panel, apply highlight colors to the selected anchor points.

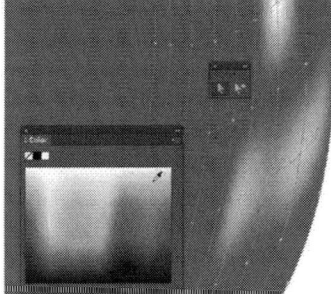

4. Experiment Using the Gradient Mesh tool involves plenty of trial and error. Have fun with it, and apply and adjust meshes to other petals.

5. If you wish, experiment with applying a gradient mesh to the leaves, as well

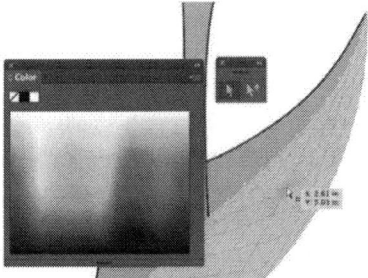

6. Save the file as an Illustrator file with default .ai file settings.

FONT PAIRING IN LOGO DESIGN

by: Brian Hoff

Know your history

Choosing a suitable and relevant font for a logo mark/symbol starts with a base understanding of history (that is too often under acknowledged).

A [good] type designer create typefaces not simply to just "look pretty." Quality typefaces were designed to fit a particular era or style in history and suited for a specific medium.

Not to say that you need to know everything there is about each typeface, but doing some history homework will take you a long way when selecting the best font solution for your logo.

Get a feel for the curves and shapes

Next time you choose a font, try zooming in close and analyzing the curves and shapes of the letter forms.

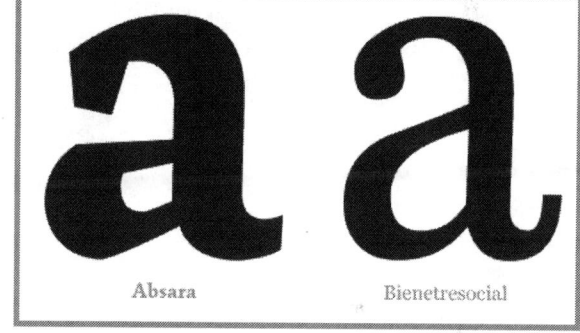

Let's compare the lowercase A's in FF Absara and Bienetresocial (free font): Absara's A has much sharper and straight curves in comparison to Bienetresocial's rounded curves. Absara's letterforms appears to be chiseled, while Bienetresocial's appears more fluid and smooth.

So what does the above have to do with pairing a logo mark with a typeface? Well, a mark that has drastic angles or points might look better with Absara because it closely mimics some of the characteristics of the typefaces, while a mark with rounded corners might look better with Bienetresocial.

Also, many designers will custom design or modify an existing typeface to help it better fit a mark and feel.

Personality

Think about the look/feel of your clients market and the overall impression you are trying to give off with your logo and pair it with a personality type (pun intended). If you cannot state a few keywords that are similar between the market, mark/symbol, and/or typeface then somewhere something needs to be adjusted, removed or modified.

A logo does not have to accompany a mark/symbol. Many of the most successful brands have beautiful, memorable logotypes that display a typeface or custom type design. Get a feel for your clients market and brainstorm what would work best.

Contrasts

Contrast
is important in design. It allows for visual differences and emphasis where needed. Try pairing thicker, more prominent marks or shapes with a thinner typeface to add atmosphere, space and/or tension.

For example, the new identity for Armani Exchange (A|X) uses a combination of thick, bold and dense boxes with a typeface that has a nice contrast of light lines to add contrast to the dense boxes and thicker lines to add relationship to the black boxes.

This is also a good example of paying attention to shape and form, as the straight, long, horizontal serifs sit perpendicular with the lines of the box. Which brings us to our next point of similarity.

Similarities

In contrast (again, pun intended) to the above, try balancing the weight of the mark to the weight of the selected typeface to create a stronger relationship.

Let's look at the example of the Exact identity. The lines of the equal (=) symbol are the same thickness of the letter form thickness of the words 'exact.' This creates a balance and relationship of the two separate elements and works to bring them together. Instead of tension we now have uniformity of elements.

Readability

When designing for any medium or subject, you should never let style get in the way of design. More importantly: style should not hinder the usability, and in our case, the readability of the typeface.

Choose a logo that works not only well at large sizes, but small sizes. Sure it might look perfectly fine at a 18-point font size on your monitor, but remember a logo will most likely appear in small corners or on business cards so it needs to be readable at very small sizes.

When testing typefaces, don't forget to shrink them down on screen in addition to printing them out at small sizes. If it's hard to read, it's most likely not the best solution.

4 GROUPS OF FONTS

by: Catherine Perry

As the choice of colors is very important for the logo design, the choice of fonts also plays an essential part in the success of a logo. Many people think a font is just a font, and they choose a font simply because they like it. As we can get feelings from colors, however, we can also get feelings from fonts too.

1-2 Serif and sans-serif fonts
Serifs are non-structural details on the ends of some of the strokes that make up letters and symbols. A font that has serifs is called 'serif font', while a font without serifs is called 'sans-serif font'. Usually words with serif font are easier to read in print, but it is harder to recognize when the size is small on the monitor. In this case, therefore, it is recommended to use sans-serif font since it doesn't have the embellishments at the end of each stroke.

3 Script fonts
A script font, as the name implies, looks like handwriting, which conveys an elegant feeling, You may find that script fonts are widely used on purfume bottles or wedding companies.

4 Decorative fonts
A decorative font entertains your eyes. They are fun and attractive. You can find them on products for children, entertainment companies etc.

A careful choice for fonts is very important, because fonts display emotions and bridge communications with the onlookers. If you are running a financial company, you need to choose a font that brings a thick and squared looks so that it makes your logo design communicate stability and security to your target clients and build confidence and trust even before they try.

> **DIFFERENT FONTS CONVEY DIFFERENT MEANINGS, THEREFORE, IT IS WISE TO SPEND SOME CAREFUL TIME ON CHOOSING A RIGHT FONT FOR A LOGO DESIGN.**

TYPOGRAPHY

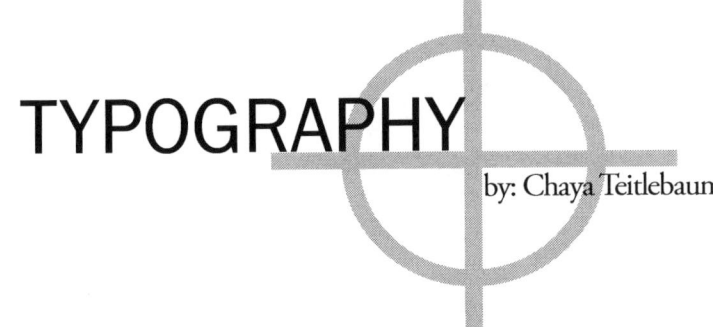

by: Chaya Teitlebaum

Serif **Aax** Sans Serif **Aax**

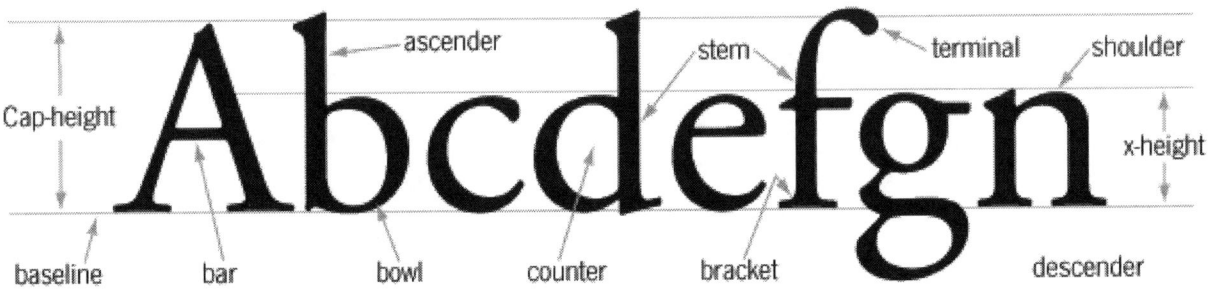

When design a logo, every nock and cranie needs to be perfect. It may be used in a HUGE size.

Here is an example of type that is set on the computer.

Walking Playing **Walking Playing**

The smaller sample looks fine. But when we look carefully at the larger sample, notice how much space is between some of the letters? You might notice the large space between the W and a in Walking. This should be tightened up by adjusting the kerning (space between letters) to make it look more professional. If you look closer, where does the kerning need more work?

Notice the extra space between the a and l in Walking, and between the a and y in Playing. Begin to train your eyes to see these small, but important areas to fix. Being able to see and fix these details is what makes a graphic designer a professional visual communicator.

Type is designed to be set at a small size (10–12 pt.) for use in books and newspapers and on the Web. When we enlarge type to make headlines, display posters, billboards, signs, etc. we must adjust the letter forms, kerning and leading so that they look good, and are legible.

Here are some examples illustrating the basics of typography that ever designer should know. Study these often, they will make your work look much more professional and developed.

Proof that we read words as shapes

I cdnuolt blveiee taht I cluod aulaclty uesdnatnrd waht I was rdanieg: the phaonmneel pweor of the hmuan mnid. Aoccdrnig to a rseearch taem at Cmabrigde Uinervtisy, it deosn't mttaer in waht oredr the ltteers in a wrod are, the olny iprmoatnt tihng is taht the frist and lsat ltteer be in the rghit pclae. The rset can be a taotl mses and you can sitll raed it wouthit a porbelm. Tihs is bcuseae the huamn mnid deos not raed ervey lteter by istlef, but the wrod as a wlohe. Such a cdonition is arppoiatrely cllaed Typoglycemia

Legibility - Pushing the Limits

The goal of any designer is to try to create something that interests the viewer and gets them to think about the message being delivered. Here are some examples of how far designers can alter the letter form and still maintain a legible message. Many customers like a challenge, so The goal of any designer is to try to create something that interests the viewer and gets them to think about the message being delivered. Here are some examples of how far designers can alter the letter form and still maintain a legible message.

Many customers like a challenge, so don't be afraid to make them think and have to work a little to get their message.

GRAND CENTRAL STATION

GRAND CENTRAL STATION

Grand Central Station

Grand Central Station

Grand Central

Grand Central

Shape

Serif type is easier to read   Sans serif type is harder to read

Black on White

Easier to read
Easier to read

Reversed

Harder to read
Harder to read

Kerning, Word Space, Tracking and Leading

Kerning
Kerning
Kerning

Word space can be adjusted
Word space can be adjusted
Word space can be adjusted

Tracking adjusts kerning and word space
Tracking adjusts kerning and word space
Tracking adjusts kerning and word space

Leading is the space between lines of type
Leading is the space between lines of type
Leading is the space between lines of type
Leading is the space between lines of type
Leading is the space between lines of type

Leading is the space between lines of type
Leading is the space between lines of type
Leading is the space between lines of type
Leading is the space between lines of type
Leading is the space between lines of type

Letterform, Font, Typeface, Type Style, and Type Family

- A letterform is the fundamental component of typographic communication—a letter, number, or mark.
  a   A   b   B   c   h   Q   s   g   2   4   8   ($?

- A font refers to a complete set of characters (letterforms) in one design, **size** and style.
  Times, 11 point, italic   **Helvetica, 11 point, bold**

- A typeface refers to the design of number and letter characters unified by consistent visual properties.
  Times   Helvetica   Della Robbia   Arial

- A type style (two words) refers to the specific style of characters of a typeface.
  Times Roman   *Times Roman Italics*   **Helvetica Black**   Della Robbia Bold

- A type family refers to the complete range of variations (styles) of a typeface design.
  Helvetica narrow   Helvetica medium   *Helvetica bold oblique*
  Helvetica narrow oblique *Helvetica oblique*   **Helvetica black**
  Helvetica light   **Helvetica bold**   ***Helvetica black oblique***
  Helvetica light oblique   **Helvetica narrow bold**

Appropriateness

One of the primary concerns designers face is whether or not their design work will "fit" into the guidelines that most viewers think a logo, or ad, or web site should look like for a particular company or industry. For example, if you are designing a logo for a bank your viewers (target market) should think, "yeah, that is what a bank logo should look like." They should feel that your design work is appropriate and fits their general idea of what a bank should look like.

Now, this isn't to say that you can't challenge their deeply held beliefs about what a bank should look like. But you may fail if it looks too different from what they expect.

Which typeface do you feel is the most appropriate for each word? Which color? the trick here is that is really depends on what your message is, and who your target market is. Wouldn't all of these work if we were talking to the right target market?

Advanced Typography - Nesting and Letter Axis

Here are examples of type design that uses the forms of various letters to help the layout and arrangement of the words. There is no right or wrong form to follow, just remind yourself that legibility is key, and that your have a message to deliver to a target audience.

THE COLOR WHEEL

The color wheel or color circle is the basic tool for combining colors. The first circular color diagram was designed by Sir Isaac Newton in 1666.

The color wheel is designed so that virtually any colors you pick from it will look good together. Over the years, many variations of the basic design have been made, but the most common version is a wheel of 12 colors based on the RYB (or artistic) color model.

Traditionally, there are a number of color combinations that are considered especially pleasing. These are called color harmonies or color chords and they consist of two or more colors with a fixed relation in the color wheel.

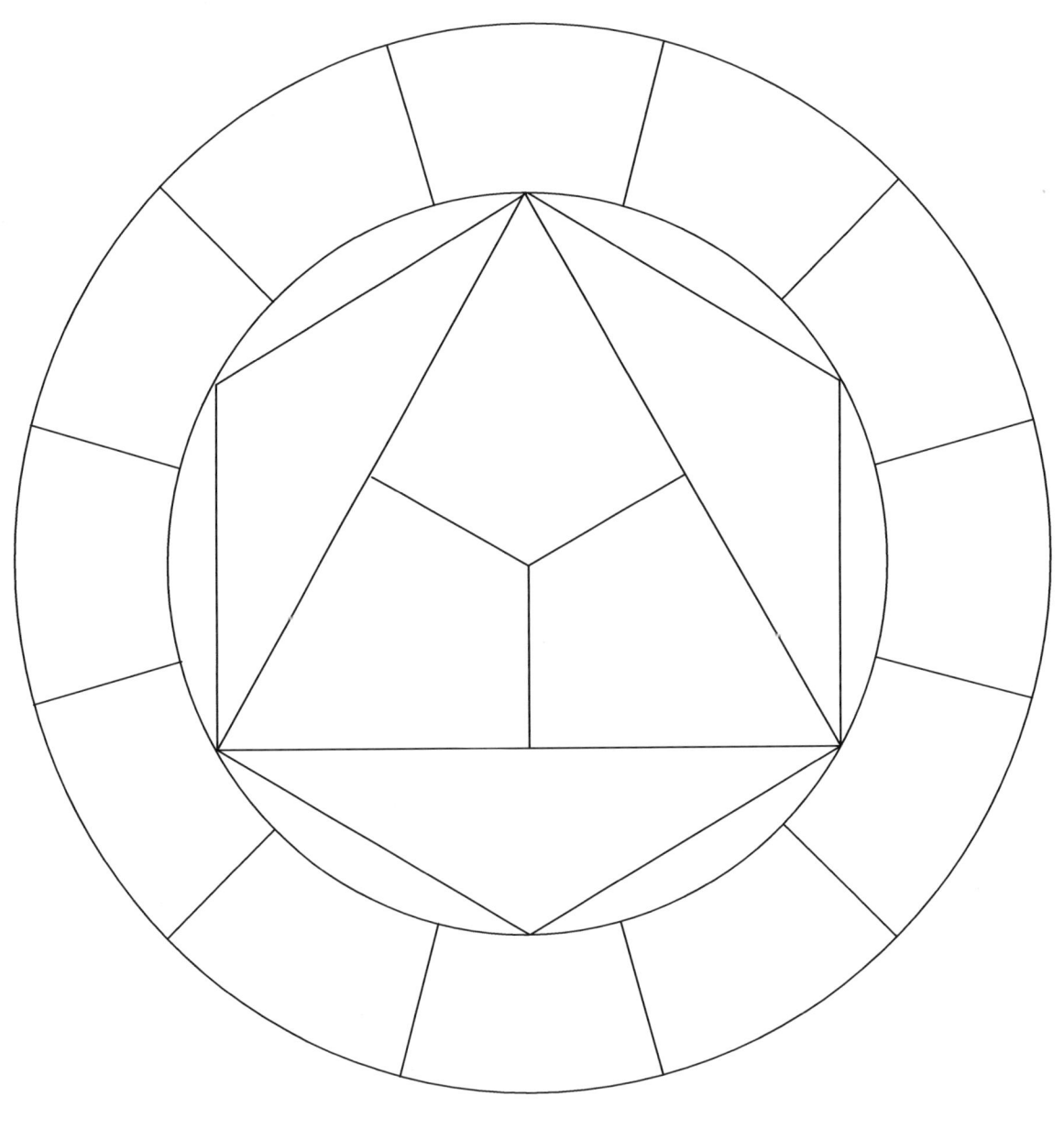

IDENTITY SETS
Standard font sizes

This is just to give you an idea of what a professional identity set can look like. Design students are often surprised just how small you can go with the type. It is important to always print out a sample as it can look very different on the screen than in print. In this sample I used Arial, fonts vary, and you will need to adjust your sizing if you are using a bigger or smaller font. Again, this is just to give you an idea, you can and should be creative and experiment.

STANDARD LETTERHEAD SIZE
US Letter 8.5 in x 11 in
European A4 210 × 297 mm
(8.3 × 11.7 in)

STANDARD BUSINESS CARD SIZE
US standard of 3.5 in x 2 in
European size 3.3 in x 2.17 in

There is a large range in envelopes the standard is probably #10 which is 9.5 in x 4.5 in.
A great resource for envelope die lines is www.designerstoolbox.com

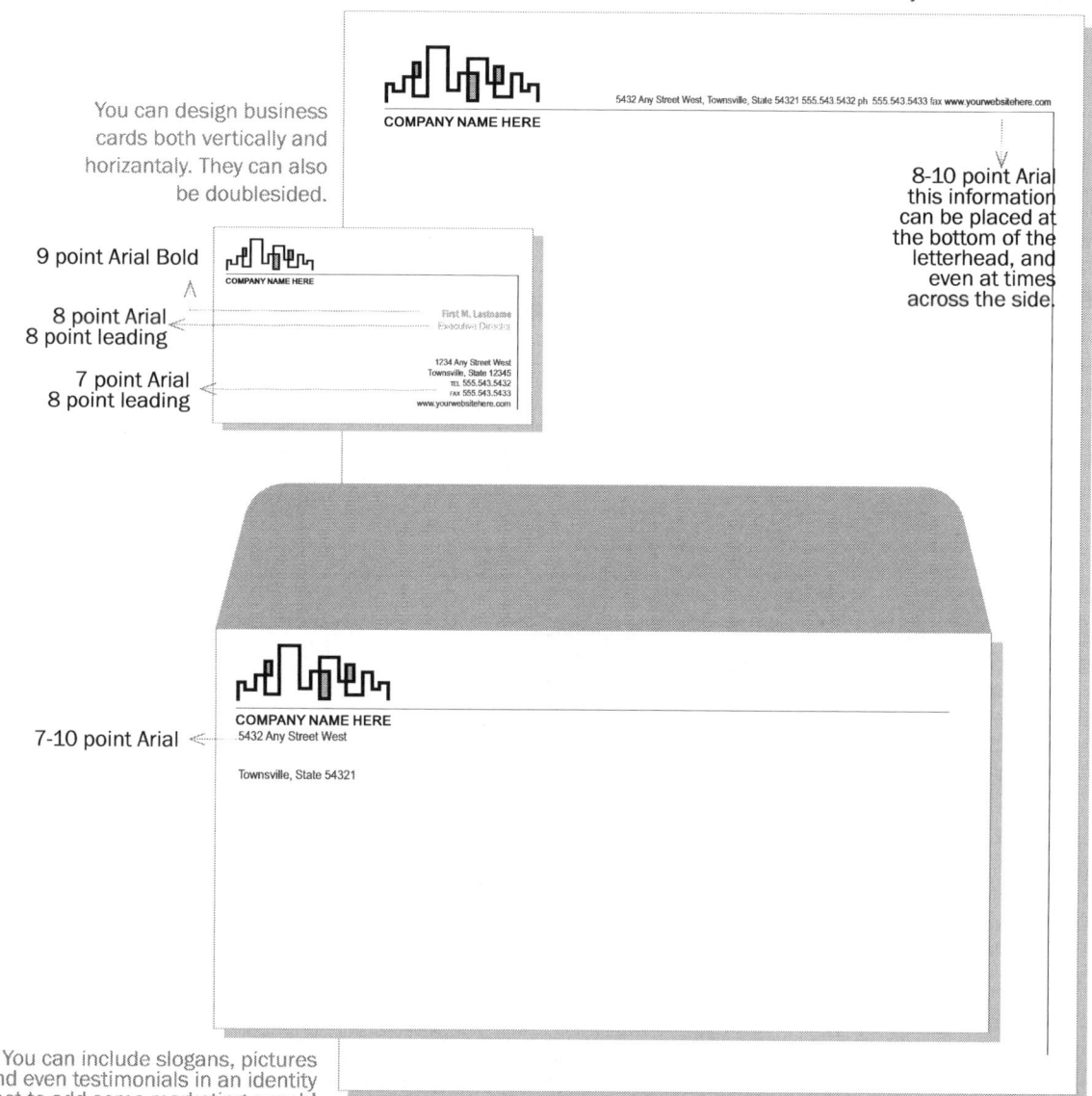

Identity Set scaled to -50%

You can design business cards both vertically and horizantaly. They can also be doublesided.

9 point Arial Bold

8 point Arial
8 point leading

7 point Arial
8 point leading

8-10 point Arial this information can be placed at the bottom of the letterhead, and even at times across the side.

7-10 point Arial

You can include slogans, pictures and even testimonials in an identity set to add some marketing punch!

Identity package

Whether designing, the first steps to developing a successful identity package is getting to know the business for which the package is intended.

About the business and its clients:
- What kind of business is it?
- What type of products or services does it produce?
- How long have they been in business?
- Who are their major competitors?
- Who needs the product or service the business produces?
- How do current or potential customers perceive the business or the industry in general?
- Does the business want to attract or focus on a specific segment of its overall customer base?

About the stationery package:
- If the business already has a stationery package in use, what do they like/dislike about the current package?
- How will the letterhead by used? (That is, will it be run through laser printers, inkjet printers, be handwritten, frequently photocopied or faxed?)
- What kind of budget does the business have and what type of volume is required?
- Will color be used? (And how much color will the budget allow?)
- Does the client have a preference for or against single, bi-fold, or tri-fold business cards, or other definite likes/dislikes?

Fonts-
- Readability is the most important thing.

Color-
- Are there established colors?
- Can you work with a colored card to start with?
- Careful use of just one color can be just effective as an entire rainbow.

Layout-
- The direction of the card can add to the design

Your design should meet all these requirements:
- The company or individual is clearly identified.
- Contact information is easy to find.
- Design reflects the client's personality.
- The pieces in the package work well together and have a unified or coordinated design.
- The letterhead design leaves ample room for the letter itself.
- The envelope meets postal regulations (placement of return address...).

"Live and breathe design daily to an obnoxious level that causes you to mentally redesign every storefront/sign/logo you see as you walk through the street"

— Mike Nelson

LOGO HISTORY

RESEARCH PROJECT Design can change the way we look at the world as well as the way the world sees us.

Joe Duffy

Research the logo design history of an established corporation—one that has been in existence for several generations. (Examples might include Shell Oil or NBC.) Through your research, note the manner in which the logos have refreshed and transformed over the entire span of the company's existence. After carefully examining this transformation, write a narrative paragraph explaining it. In your writing, use visually descriptive language, replete with metaphors and evocative adjectives. To help you truly articulate what you see, pretend you are describing this visual evolution to a visually impaired friend.

LOGO EVOLUTION

by: Jonathan Munk

Evolution is a process of change or development. It is when one version of a product is better than the previous one. This type of change was first catalogued by Darwin over a hundred years ago in the Galapagos Islands. But in the truest sense, evolution occurs in nearly every aspect of our lives, and especially in the business and consumer worlds. It seems that companies find themselves needing to be fast-paced, up-to-date and ever evolving to stay ahead of the competition.

But does a company commit an unpardonable sin by deciding to alter their identity, their mainstay–their logo?

If you think about the world's most prominent brands, Nike, McDonalds, Coca-Cola and others, it is easy to visualize their respective logos. Those designs have become the visual representation of the company brand, which is what people think about your company and their experiences with it. So, does that mean a logo should never be changed in order to avoid customer alienation and mistrust?

Believe it or not, logo evolution is as common as evolution in any other part of business, but to a lesser degree. Although drastic changes in a logo design can cause alienation and mistrust among existing and potential customers, never changing a logo can also have an adverse effect as well. While a logo update from time to time tells customers that the company is staying up-to-date in its offerings and still knows how to connect with its customers, a logo that never changes can make customers feel like the company is out of touch with its clientele.

ALTHOUGH DRASTIC CHANGES IN A LOGO DESIGN CAN CAUSE ALIENATION AND MISTRUST AMONG EXISTING AND POTENTIAL CUSTOMERS, NEVER CHANGING A LOGO CAN ALSO HAVE AN ADVERSE EFFECT.

Of course, changes should be subtle and keep the same basic design elements so the logo can still be easily associated with the company, product or service. Change should not occur too often either, as this can give an impression of a company without clear vision. There is a delicate balance, but in most cases it is appropriate to prudently alter a company logo from time to time.

You'd probably be surprised to find out just how many companies have made changes to their logo without you even knowing. This is logo evolution. It takes place over decades and the changes are subtle.

LOGO EVOLUTION

by: Jonathan Munk

 1955

SONY 1957

SONY 1961

SONY 1962

SONY 1969

SONY 1973

SONY
The four letters that make up this company logo have seemingly gone unchanged since the company began. But look at the images below. Aside from the company's first rendition, the logo has changed very little, with most alterations occurring in letter height and boldness.

NIKE
Nike's world famous swoosh was designed by Portland State University student Caroline Davidson in 1971. She was paid just $35 for her design (Source: Nike.com), which, even with inflation, is unreal in the graphic design world. The design has undergone very few changes over the years, but there have been definite changes to the logo over the years. Nike also has variations on the logo for its different divisions, like Nike Skate and Nike Soccer.

The evolution of logos only applies to companies that aren't seeking to reinvent themselves. Businesses that feel they aren't building relationships with their target markets may need a logo makeover and reposition themselves.

But when updates and alterations are appropriate, be sure the changes need are understated, gradual and done with the consumer in mind. Companies that update their logos in conjunction with corporate evolution will be building trust and staying fresh in the minds of consumers, as long as the changes are subtle instead of staggering.

UNIT THREE
LAYOUT

MOODBOARDS
create two!

TONE:
What tone are you working on achieving? Write three keywords as adjectives for the tone of your project.

INSPIRATION:
Look on www.pinterest.com, www.dieline.com and other sites where you can look at beautiful projects. Choose at least 3 images as inspiration for your project.

IMAGES:
Choose the style images that you might use for your project. Are they isolated on white? Action images? Texture? Scale?
Choose 3 images in the style you are considering.

COLOR PALATE:
Choose the color palate for your project your color palate should have 3 colors, in some cases you can use more than 3 colors.
- You can go to www.color.adobe.com and use their explore option and put in some related keywords for ideas and inspiration.
- You can use the "create" option on www.color.adobe.com, to create your own color theme. You can start by working with the color of your logo and using the color rules that we learnt (triadic, complementary...)
- You can choose a color palate based on inspiration of an object or design that you have come across.

TYPOGRAPHY:
Choose a font for your headings and a font for your body text.
- You can choose a typography based on inspiration of an object or design that you have come across.
- Remember that for your body text the most important thing is legibility, so you might think that the typography for your body text is boring and that OK.
- Remember that simple is often better, you don't need to go font happy :)
- Some good sites to find free fonts are www.fontsquirrel.com and www.losttype.com

Compile all these elements in an InDesign document and PDF it.

quick review!
TO SET UP A TRIFOLD BROCHURE IN INDESIGN.

SET UP THE BROCHURE IN INDESIGN
1. File>new
2. Choose "print"
3. Choose your paper size, I'm choosing A4.

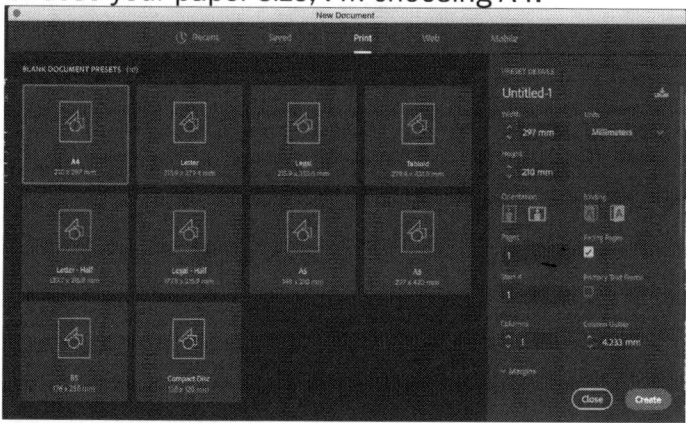

4. We need to divide the landscape part of our paper into 3 sections. Choose your orientation to be landscape, take the measurement that they have for the width and divide it into 3.
5. In this case I'm taking 297mm/3=99mm.
   (If you are doing a letter size paper, each page will be 3.6666in since that's 11in/3 in)
   Note: it automatically changes your orientation to portrait and that's ok.
6. Choose 6 pages since you're counting the front and back panels.
   Choose 2 columns, since that's the standard grid for a trifold.
7. You can change your margins depending on your look. (I'm choosing .375in or 9.5cm)
8. Add a bleed of .125in or 3mm
9. Click "create", your document will appear, now it may look awkward as it comes in sets of two. We're going to change that.

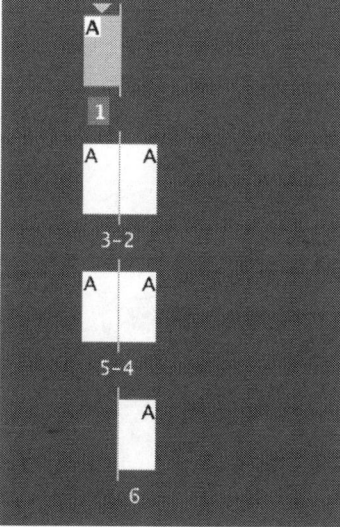

TO SET UP A TRIFOLD BROCHURE IN INDESIGN.

SET UP THE BROCHURE IN INDESIGN
1. File>new
2. Choose "print"
3. Choose your paper size, I'm choosing A4.

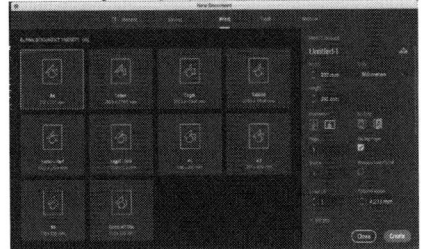

4. We need to divide the landscape part of our paper into 3 sections. Choose your orientation to be landscape, take the measurement that they have for the width and divide it into 3.
5. In this case I'm taking 297mm/3=99mm.
   (If you are doing a letter size paper, each page will be 3.6666in since that's 11in/3 in)
   Note: it automatically changes your orientation to portrait and that's ok.
6. Choose 6 pages since you're counting the front and back panels.
   Choose 2 columns, since that's the standard grid for a trifold.
7. You can change your margins depending on your look. (I'm choosing .375in or 9.5cm)
8. Add a bleed of .125in or 3mm
9. Click "create", your document will appear, now it may look awkward as it comes in sets of two. We're going to change that.

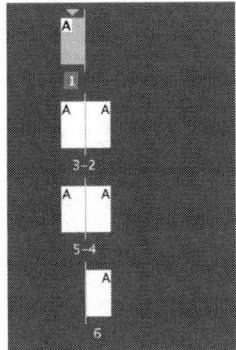

10. In your pages panel, select all your pages by holding down Shift and clicking on the first and last one.
11. Right click, and choose "allow document pages to shuffle" and "allow document spreads to shuffle". They should both not be checked off. (Don't ask me why that makes sense!)

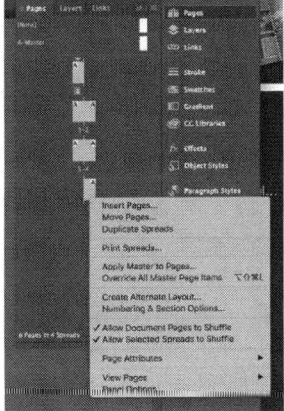

12. You can select each page and move them near each other. (You will see a bracket appear)

yay! your trifold is set up!

quick review!
WHAT IS EACH PANEL FOR?

After you set it up you have 3 panels on each spread. What are they for?
Take a peice of paper and fold it in three to better follow along.
Write on them what each panel is for and it will bacome clearer. Then, type it in your indesign file so that you know exactly what goes where.

Here's an example:

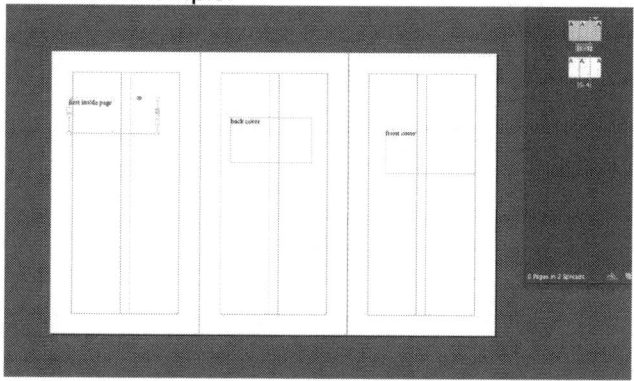

Here's an example with the design:

inside page folded in   back cover   cover

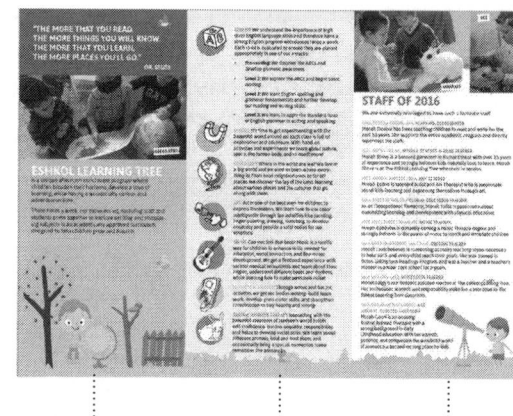

inside page 1   inside page 2   inside page 3

Here's what it will look like once folded:

cover   inside page 1   inside page 2   inside page folded in

TYPOGRAPHY TIPS

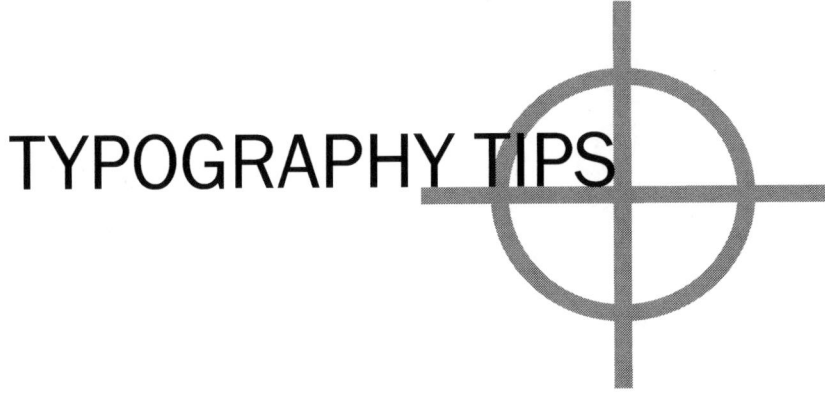

SERIF TEXT WITH A SANS SERIF HEADLINE
Serif text is almost always the better choice for body text in brochure printing. Serif fonts are the ones that have little "feet" or lines jutting out from the end of each letter. Examples: Times New Roman, Georgia. Sans Serif fonts, like Arial and Gill Sans, work better as headlines because headline text is larger and sans serif fonts are hard to read at small sizes.

USE CONTRASTING STYLES
Using Serif and Sans Serif fonts for different elements is also recommended because similar typefaces don't offer enough contrast and will therefore cause a visual clash. Using two script fonts for a headline and subheads won't work because there isn't enough of a difference for readers to tell which is a headline, and therefore a new subject, and which is a subhead.

DON'T USE TOO MANY FONTS
A lot of people are font happy. Just because their computer comes with 100 fonts, they feel as though they need to use each one in a single brochure. Fight this urge! Limit your number of fonts to three or four (two is actually preferred – one Serif and one Sans Serif) so that your brochure has a consistent look throughout. Changing from one font to another to another can make a brochure look like it's from multiple companies instead of one company trying to forge a brand message.

THE TEXT SHOULDN'T BLEND IN WITH THE BACKGROUND
Use dark text on a light background to ensure readability. You can use white on a black background, but it's harder on the eyes when the background is darker than the text. Just make sure not to use a light color like yellow on a light background, like light green.

SIZE
Set body text in 9-12 pt. type.
The leading should be 2-5 points higher than the font size.

CAPTION TEXT
- Set captions in a different typeface.
- Vary the weight of captions rather than making them too small (for instance setting captions in italics rather than 6 pt. type.)
- After to the cover, captions are the most read portions of a brochure; they must be readable.

GENERAL TEXT GUIDELINES
- Use graphical dingbats like bullets to break up the text
- Minimize the use of caps, italics, and bold
- Consider using color to vary appearance and call attention to specific items
- Be consistent (set all headlines in one typeface and style, all captions in one typeface and style, and so on)

PROOFING CHECKLIST

Duz it realy mater if there are a cuple of mistaiks in ur work?

- Spelling
- Grammar
- Facts (time, date)
- Contact Info
- Call for Action
- Fonts
- Graphics/Message Ratio
- Project in Context
- Test Run
- CMYK
- Indicia
- Bleed/Crop Marks
- Size

"This is the very perfection of a man, to find out his own imperfections."

INDEPENDENT PROJECT

PROJECT PROPOSAL

> Design can change the way we look at the world as well as the way the world sees us.
>
> Joe Duffy

Choose something of interest to you. Make sure it is something you have enough time and resources to complete entire project by the deadline provided. This project can be for a real company or a fictitious one that strikes you fancy. The bulk of this project will be done on your own. This is your opportunity to show your stuff, go ahead; Impress yourselves and impress us.

Ex. Packaging, Magazine Layout, Advertisement, Invitation, Billboard, Poster, Book cover or anything else you can think of.

- What will I work towards producing?

- Who is my target audience? (social, economic group? age?)

- What research do I need to do? (Primary, Secondary)

- What resources do I need? Where will I get them from?

- What tools/programs will I use?

- How will know my work is going in the right direction? (surveys...)

- Can I meet the deadline? (create a timescale for yourselves)

Good luck.

EVALUATION

- Explain your task
- Why did you choose this subject
- What interested you about this subject
- (Who is your target audience)
- Show your development from your brief through the completion of your package
- Describe your research
- Explain how you went about researching for your project (shops, newspapers, websites)
- Describe what you sketched and how your ideas developed from a sketch to a tangible thing
- Explain the programs your used and why
- Advantages and disadvantages
- Talk about what limited you in this project (time, resources, limitations of software etc)
- Briefly explain what effects you used and the methods you used to create your project and describe the challenges you faced along the way
- Why did you choose that particular style layout
- Did you enjoy this project, are you proud of your results and what do you feel you walked away with

WHAT'S IN AN AD?

Look around your house to find an ad in a newspaper or magazine. Look at the ad, then answer the questions below. Attach your ad to this worksheet and bring it to class.

1. Where did you find the ad?

2. Who is responsible for the ad? (Hint: Look for a logo—a symbol used by companies to identify their products.)

3. What is the ad trying to get you to buy, do, or think?

4. Who is the ad meant for (the target audience)? What makes you think so?

5. What do you think about the ad? Does it make you want to buy the product? Why or why not?

6. What does the ad say about the people who buy the product or service?

CREATING AN AD

adapted from Pete Barry

KISS: **K**eep **I**t **S**imple **S**tupid- meaning get to the point
SLIP IT:
Smile: Disarms you
Laugh: Really disarms you
Informs: tells you something you don't know
Provokes: a reaction and an emotional response
Involves, there's a connection and an interaction and it makes you **Thinks**

What do you want to say?

Who are you talking to?

How do you want to say it?

STRATEGIES

adapted from Pete Barry

Strategy → Concept • Idea → Campaign • Tagline → Executions

1. Before and After
2. Before Only
3. After Only
4. Advice
5. Knowledge
6. Empathy
7. Demonstration
8. Testimonial
9. Heritage
10. Owner or Staff
11. Product Positioning
12. Competitive or Comparison
13. Challenge
14. Negative to Positive
15. Logic
16. Price- Cheap or expensive
17. Honesty

OGILVY ON ADVERTISING

from his book
"Ogilvy On Advertising"

WHO IS DAVID OGILVY AND WHY SHOULD WE LISTEN TO HIM?
- David Ogilvy is commonly called "The Father of Advertising".
- He was referred to as "the most sought after wizard in today's advertising industry", Time Magazine, 1962.
- He started his company Ogilvy, Benson & Mather in 1948 with $6,000 and sold it in 1989 for $864 million.
- Adweek magazine asked people in the business "Which individuals—alive or dead—made you consider pursuing a career in advertising?" Ogilvy topped the list. And the same result came when students of advertising were surveyed. His best-selling book "Confessions of an Advertising Man" is one of the most popular and famous books on advertising.

1. RESULTS ARE MORE IMPORTANT THAN TRYING TO BE ORIGINAL OR CREATIVE

"I do not regard advertising as entertainment or an art form but as a medium of information. When I write an advertisement, I don't want you to tell me that you find it "creative". I want you to find it so interesting that you buy the product. When Aeschines spoke, they said "How well he speaks." But when Demosthenes spoke, they said "Let us march against Philip".

Good advertising results in people taking action i.e. People buy your product, service or idea.

2. MAKE DECISIONS BASED ON RESEARCH NOT GUT INSTINCT

"I am sometimes attacked for imposing "rules". Nothing could be further from the truth. I hate rules. All I do is report on how consumers react to different stimuli. I may say to a copywriter "Research shows that commercials with celebrities are below average in persuading people to buy products. Are you sure you want to use a celebrity?" Call that a rule? Or I may say to an art director "Research suggests that if you set the copy in black type on a white background, more people will read it than if you set it in white type on a black background". A hint perhaps but scarcely a rule."

Research shows you what works and what doesn't work, do what works, don't do what doesn't work.

3. CREATE BIG IDEAS THAT SELL

"You can do homework from now until doomsday but you will never win fame and fortune unless you also invent big ideas. It takes a big idea to attract the attention of consumers and get them to buy your product. Unless your advertising contains a big idea, it will pass like a ship in the night."

Big ideas make people gasp when they see it, make people wish they had thought of it themselves, are unique, fit into the overall strategy and last for a long time.

4. BETTER IS NOT ENOUGH

"If you and your competitors all make excellent products don't try to imply that your product is better. Just say what is good about your product

The great advertising pioneer David Ogilvy ran through 18 concepts for shirt-maker client Hathaway's ad campaign before deciding on Baron Wrangell, "The Man with the Eye Patch."

Hathaway had been making shirts for 116 years, but was little noticed. This ad, with the mysterious character in the eye patch, instantly catapulted Hathaway as the #1 selling dress shirt in the world.

and do a clearer, more honest, more informative job of saying it."
Everyone says that their product is "better", "better" is generic, specifics are what differentiate you from your competitors.
Don't just say that your product is better, prove it.

5. LET YOUR WINNERS RUN

"If you are lucky enough to write a good advertisement, repeat it until it stops selling. Scores of good advertisements have been discarded before they lost their potency."
Often advertising is removed in favour of something fresh and new because of the appointment of a new advertising agency or managing director therefore replacing something that is potentially working very well with something that doesn't work.
It helps to test the new advertising against the old under similar conditions to be certain that the new advertising is actually better.

6. WRITE HEADLINES THAT SELL THE COPY

"On the average, five times as many people read the headlines as read the body copy. It follows that unless your headline sells your products, you have wasted 90 per cent of your money."
People are busy, they rarely open a magazine or newspaper and read it from cover to cover, instead they skim through the major headlines until they come across something that interests them.
People won't read what you have to say if the headline doesn't answer the question "what's in it for me?"

7. YOU CAN'T BORE PEOPLE INTO BUYING YOUR PRODUCT

"You can not bore people into buying your product. You can only interest them into buying it."
People are motivated by emotions and they justify with logic.
Logic alone does not motivate people into taking action.

"The consumer is not a moron, she's your wife! Don't insult her intelligence. You wouldn't lie to your wife, don't lie to mine."

— David Ogilvy

OGILVY STYLE
MODERN SAMPLES

David felt that the advertising business had changed with the introduction of these creative awards contests. I mean the advertising business is maybe one of the few businesses where people give awards to each other. And on what basis do they do it? Because they like it, because it's entertaining. He gave this speech saying, " There's a disease called entertainment, that's infecting our business." I think he didn't recognize that a lot of the advertising today must be entertaining to get a younger generation to pay attention. But for him, the measure of an advertisement's success was always its ability to sell.

PRACTICAL LAYOUT

By Jacci Howard Bear

WHEN READERS LOOK AT YOUR AD WHAT DO THEY SEE FIRST? RESEARCH INDICATES THAT READERS TYPICALLY LOOK AT:

- Visual
- Caption
- Headline
- Copy
- Signature (Advertisers name, contact information)

in that order.

One method of making sure your ad gets read is to arrange elements in that order, top to bottom. However, your ad should also lead with its strongest element. Sometimes the visual may be secondary to the headline. In that case you may decide to put the headline first. A caption may not be necessary at all times and often you'll want to include additional elements such as secondary illustrations or a coupon box.

"I don't know the rules of grammar... If you're trying to persuade people to do something, it seems to me you should use their language, the language they use every day, the language in which they think. We try to write in the vernacular."

While this isn't the only way to design an ad, it is an easy to implement, successful formula for many types of products or services. David Ogilvy who used this layout formula for some of his most successful ads.

BASIC OGILVY AD LAYOUT

Advertising expert David Ogilvy devised an ad layout formula for some of his most successful ads that became known as the Ogilvy. The illustration on this page is the basic design that follows the classic visual, headline, caption, copy, signature format. From this basic ad layout, other variations are derived.

Try changing the margins, fonts, leading, size of the initial cap, size of the visual, and placing the copy in columns to customize the basic format of this ad layout.

- **VISUAL** at the top of the page. If you are using a photo, bleed it to the edge of the page or ad space for maximum impact.
- For photos, place a descriptive **CAPTION** below.
- Put your **HEADLINE** next.
- Follow with your main ad **COPY**. Consider a drop cap as a lead-in to help draw the reader into the copy.
- Place your contact information (**SIGNATURE**) in the lower right corner. That's generally the last place a reader's eye gravitates to when reading an ad.

DO WE READ?

ThinkEyeTracking.com

Some months ago I was discussing the demise of long copy advertisements on a train journey with Rory Sutherland: I asked him if thought the amount of time we spend online had shortened our attention spans and if this had led to the demise of long copy ads?

"Oh no my dear boy!" Boomed the reply. "The decline began long before that, you see the problem stems from when the industry started to place more emphasis on art and less on the copy, this happened at least ten years before the internet came into its own."

I was encouraged by Rory's response and wanted to test if people would still engage with long copy adverts. As good fortune would have it I found a I copy of Good Housekeeping from the late 90's whilst on holiday in France. Whilst flicking through it I found an interesting long copy ad from BT. I 'borrowed' the magazine and included the BT advert as part of a ThinkPrint Advertising Effectiveness omnibus study.

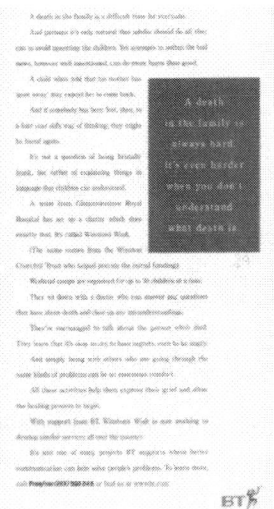

Above: Double page spread from Good House Keeping 1999.

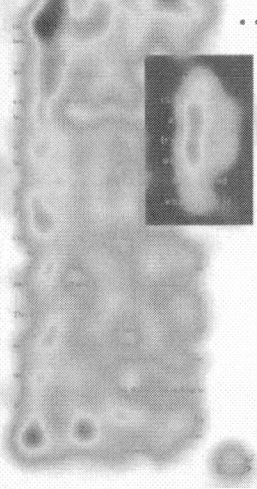

As you can see in the heat map (based on thirty female respondents who viewed the creative in the context of a magazine whilst being eye tracked), the long copy ad worked. Rory was right, the internet hadn't rotted our brains between 1999 and 2010, long copy ads had simply fallen out of fashion.

EYE TRACKING HEATMAPS SHOWS MAGAZINE READERS FROM 2010 ARE PREPARED TO READ LONG COPY ADVERTS.

HOW TO DESIGN A BILLBOARD AD

by Randy Ruggles

1. Know your product and its target audience. You can design a beautiful billboard, but if it's not attracting the people who will buy your product, it's absolutely useless. Knowing your audience is important in deciding the ad design and picking a location for the billboard.

2. Showcase the product up front. You can't tease your viewers like radio and tv ads do, because they'll only see the ad for a few seconds. They need to know immediately what you're selling. Your product or service should be the largest image in the ad.

3. Keep the layout simple. Again, the viewers won't have a lot of time to read a complicated message. It must be short and focus solely on the product.

4. Make the ad stand out. If you want your ad to be noticed, the billboard can't blend in with its surroundings. Use bright vibrant colors with a high contrast so it will be highly visible.

5. Send a message that will get people's attention. Design a short message (eight words or less is good) that will stick in their heads. Using humor and intrigue always works, but remember that it must still associate with the product.

IMPORTANT!
Speak to your printer because when printing on plastics and large sizes printers vary...

SETTING UP A DOCUMENT
With billboards, we usually give an inch for each foot at 300 dpi. Because you view it from so far, it does not need to be the same dpi as a brochure. Again... speak to the printer.

The billboard's location can be key. If it's downtown and viewed by slower drivers and pedestrians, you may be able to use a longer message than if the billboard is on a freeway. However, always keep the message simple.

UNIT FOUR
BUSINESS

What I wish they taught me in design school

How to design for your worst client: YOURSELF!

SELF PROMOTION

by: Mark Bowley

As a graphic designer a portfolio is essential. While the website is the most important, it's also a good idea to have a physical one too to take along to meetings and interviews.

Putting together and showing this kind of portfolio of your graphic design work is quite a skill, and the best way to do it gets debated constantly by designers around the world. There is no right way of doing it – there will always be differences in what employers or clients expect, or would like to see. Some simple logic and advice will help you though.

YOUR AUDIENCE. Who will be looking at it?

As designers, when we start a design project one of the first questions we always ask is who the audience will be. You should be applying the same thinking when putting together your portfolio – who will be looking at it? What are their needs and expectations? Depending on your situation, your target audience is likely to be one of the following:

- A potential employer
- A potential client

If you are looking for a job in the design industry remember potential employers will most likely be designers themselves. This means they will have a keen eye for the look of your work and will want to understand your contribution to each project.

If you are looking for work from potential clients they, on the other hand, will be more focussed on whether you have experience in the type of work they need to produce, and whether your design style is to their taste.

ADAPT WHERE YOU CAN

Try to adapt your portfolio and presentation style to fit each audience. This means a bit more work each time but will make it more engaging for them. It will also lead to more success for you by demonstrating you understand their business.

2 CHOOSING PROJECTS. Only select your best work.

LIMIT THE NUMBER
If you can, try and keep it to about 6-15 good size projects. People don't want to go through everything you have done and will probably make up their minds about you during the first 3 you show. Obviously if you don't have much to show for any of them (e.g an individual logo) you could consider showing more projects.

SELECT YOUR BEST
I can't stress this one enough and you will hear the same thing from other people in the industry: Only select your best work and work you want to talk about. If you don't love it or can't talk about it endlessly, over and over, it will show and they won't be interested. I know myself it's tempting to fill out your portfolio with work that isn't your best but shows other skills or types of client. But it won't be long before you struggle to talk about them engagingly, and you will come across as not enjoying your work.

> **"PEOPLE DON'T WANT TO GO THROUGH EVERYTHING YOU HAVE DONE AND WILL PROBABLY MAKE UP THEIR MINDS ABOUT YOU DURING THE FIRST 3 YOU SHOW."**

WHAT ORDER TO SHOW THEM IN?
The first and last projects in your portfolio will stick in people's minds the most. So, you should select carefully which projects to put in these positions. In addition, the last project can be the best place for a project you really like talking about or has samples that people can look at. This is because it can often end up staying open on the desk while you continue the meeting.

The projects you show in the middle of your portfolio should then be ordered in a way that demonstrates variety in skills and style. Keep them interested by mixing things up and being dramatic. If there are samples to pass around for one project, consider following it with a project that doesn't. Don't, for example, put all your logo or brochure projects back to back if you can help it.

SHOW CREATIVITY
One of the things potential employers will often look for is how you got to the finished design. They may be interested in sketch books, loosely bound sheets of ideas, mood boards or unused concepts. Put a few of them in your portfolio but not for every project. They are there to demonstrate your ability to think and and sketch before you jumped on a Mac to create the work.

You should also aim to include at least one or two mockups or printed samples. This will stop your portfolio from looking like just a collection of flat printouts of your work, and therefore a more memorable experience.

less is more!

PUT IN WHAT YOU WANT TO GET OUT

What does this mean? Well one important thing to remember is that you should only put types of work in your portfolio that you want to get more of. If you've done a lot of one type of work but you're now really tired of it, don't put it in your portfolio even if you think it's good work. Chances are, you will only get more of it.

PRESENTATION IS KEY

The standard of presentation in your portfolio must be the highest you can achieve. Employers and clients alike will be judging how much attention you pay to these details as well as the actual work. But don't dress it up – the quality of your work and your presentation is much more important than a fancy or tricksy portfolio.

Brand Yourself. The brand you create shouldn't be based on only design elements (logo and colors). It should reflect your personality and the way you want to express yourself. It might be bold and modern, with an element of surprise. You can take that and build a brand design around that. Your brand is personal, it should come from you and not something you've seen. Trends mostly die so avoid those at all costs.

3 EXPLAINING THE WORK

OK, so we have covered putting your portfolio together, but you also need to learn how to talk about it.

It's not easy

The art of talking about your work is not something that comes naturally to designers – I know I didn't find it easy in the beginning. But it's a good skill to learn, and learn as early as you can. Don't be afraid of making mistakes and look upon each meeting as an opportunity to develop this skill. Not only will this make it easier to talk about your portfolio, it will also make you better at presenting concepts and design work, both to your colleagues and to clients.

The simple rule here is engagement. Your aim should be to arouse interest in your work, not give a speech or lecture. Remember, showing your portfolio to people is also about them, not just you.

When you come to each project, talk about it briefly to introduce it but don't talk at length. See how they react, let them ask questions or let them simply look. If they are looking at you rather than the work, talk some more about the project – tell them what interested you about it. Look for signs that it's time to move on to the next project.

To help you get used to talking about your work, try it on other people whenever you get a chance. If they are non-designers it will help even more, as you will practice not using designer lingo to describe each project.

> **FOCUS LESS ON TALKING UP THE DESIGN AESTHETICS OF YOUR WORK, AND MORE ON EXPLAINING THE VALUE OF YOUR SERVICES TO THE CLIENT OF EACH PROJECT**

SHOW YOUR VALUE

Employers want to see how you could be useful in their organisation, and when showing your portfolio they will often ask what your involvement was on a project. Whatever you are tempted to say, I advise this: Be honest, give yourself credit, but be clear about your skills.

A potential client will be wanting to find out if you have the skills they currently need. Focus less on talking up the design aesthetics of your work, and more on explaining the value of your services to the client of each project. Were they pleased with the work? Did they achieve their business goals?

KNOW YOURSELF

You should take some time to understand your strengths and weaknesses (and yes, we all have weaknesses) before showing your work. If you can't see them yourself ask another designer for an honest opinion (and be prepared for the answers!). You may not get asked about these specifically in a meeting, but you should be prepared to discuss them anyway.

The reason I mention this is that showing you understand your limits and where you are most effective is far better than trying to prove you are simply amazing. Employers and clients are interested in how they can use you best – they know no-one is good at everything and are not looking for that.

If you are particularly strong in one area though, make sure every piece of work in your portfolio shows that without you even having to say it. They will remember you better that way.

GRAPHIC DESIGN INTERVIEW TIPS

by Lee Newham, a senior designer at London-based design consultancy, P&W.

⊕ When you arrive in the interview give us your business card. It should be well designed, memorable, simple and hopefully have a great idea. It should be unique and you should be branded.

⊕ Have 8–12 pieces of work in your folio. Put the best pieces at the front and back.

Have at least six questions ready to ask (if you have less, you'll find they will be answered in the course of the interview).

⊕ Take a pad and pen, take it out at the beginning of the interview. You don't have to take notes, but it looks as if you are organized.

⊕ Talk about your work before you show it, but don't talk too much. This should be one short sentence to engage the interviewer with you. We will be looking at you as you speak. Then show us your work.

Have samples and mock ups.

⊕ Bring sketches. We are as interested in how you got to the final solution as the solution itself. You can show other concepts.

> "In order to be irreplaceable one must always be different."
> —Coco Chanel

⊕ Have a copy of your CV (resumé) at the back of the portfolio. Offer it even if we already have it.

On your CV don't tell people about exam results or part-time jobs that have nothing to do with your chosen career.

⊕ Don't talk about holiday or money in a first interview.

⊕ Tell us you really want the job (believe it or not, hardly anyone does this).

⊕ When you get back home, send an email thanking us for the interview.

⊕ Make sure your branding is consistent on your business card, CV and email signature.

sources: *Burn Your Portfolio* by Michael Janda

THE FIXED-BID PRICING DARTBOARD

Trying to determine how to price your work fairly can be a daunting task. In my experience, most clients prefer working with fixed-bid pricing; they take comfort in knowing exactly what they are going to get for exactly what price. On the designer side, there is comfort in knowing exactly what you are going to charge for the scope of work.

Fixed-bid pricing presents several challenges, not the least of which is the fact that you have to base your price on something. When I first started freelancing, that something was often hours. I decided to charge around $XX per hour for my time, and then I would ballpark my hours and send an estimate to my client. The problem with this pricing technique was that I am a very fast designer and production artist. So by charging based on hours, I was charging too little for most of the work I was producing. That left me in a situation where I either needed to up my hourly rate or figure out a new way to price my work.

I began trying to price things based on the deliverables.

My estimates would include itemized pricing for each of the elements being produced. For a website, for example. I would charge $500 for a homepage and $150 for each subpage. Then I'd add up all the pages and come up with a price. It didn't take me too long to learn (the hard way) that this strategy was riddled with problems. After experimenting with other strategies, I realized that there is no perfect science to estimating your work. It frequently seems as if you are throwing a dart at a board and seeing where it lands. In some ways this is true. With fixed-bid pricing, you are often throwing out a dart and hoping you land on the board in a quadrant that will generate a profit. While there is no perfect method to estimating your work, there is a strategy to make sure you are throwing your dart toward the right area of the board. Let's examine each component of fixed-bid pricing: cost, value, and budget

sources: Burn Your Portfolio by Michael Janda

PRICING STRATEGIES: FIXED BID

Fixed-bid pricing is a set scope of work with a specific price. You tell the clients exactly what you are going to do and exactly what the cost will be. As long as the clients stay within the scope of the project, they are charged the price you quoted. In my experience, fixed-bid pricing is the option most commonly used in the graphic design industry.

DESIGNER

Pros

- You know exactly what you are going to make on the project.
- If the job takes you less time than you expected, you make more profit.

Cons

- Since you are locked into a price, if the job takes you more time than expected, you make less profit (or even lose money).

CLIENT

Pros

- The clients know exactly what they are going to have to pay assuming they stay within the project scope.
- They can reasonably assume that they will be able to stay within their allocated budget for the project.

Cons

- Due to the tricky nature of fixed-bid pricing, you as the design agency will often need to pad your estimate to account for any unforeseen challenges in the project. As a result, the clients could end up paying a lot more for a project than if it were priced in a different structure.
- If the clients go out of the scope to a degree that requires you to send them change orders, they can become frustrated and feel like you are nickel-and-diming them.

⚠ ISSUES TO WATCH OUT FOR:

With fixed-bid pricing you must clearly define the scope of the project. If you don't have every minute detail (deliverables, functionality, design rounds, change rounds, and so on) defined in your proposal, there is a high likelihood that you will eventually get stung by a fixed-bid project.

ou must try to help the clients adhere to the defined project scope. Unfortunately, no matter what you do to clearly detail the project, there is a chance that the clients will come up with something they want you to do that was not included in your scope. Keeping them in scope can be a challenging client-management task.

WHEN TO USE IT:

Fixed-bid structures are best used when clients know exactly what they want you to produce and exactly what they are comfortable spending.

sources: Burn Your Portfolio by Michael Janda

PRICING STRATEGIES: HOURLY

You and your clients agree on an hourly rate. You track your hours and bill your clients in regularly agreed-upon intervals (such as weekly or monthly).

DESIGNER

Pros

◈ For every hour you spend on a project, you have something to bill for. This structure eliminates the risk of losing money on a project.

Cons

◈ Value pricing doesn't come into play in this structure. If you design a logo in one hour, you are locked into charging your clients the agreed-upon hourly rate even though the value of the logo to the clients far exceeded what they paid for it.

CLIENT

Pros

◈ Clients do not need a clearly defined project scope to begin working with you.

◈ They have the lexibility to change their mind about their needs and add new items to your plate.

Cons

◈ It can be difficult for the clients to know how much they should budget for your services if they are paying by the hour.

⚠ ISSUES TO WATCH OUT FOR:

To help keep your relationships with your clients healthy, you should regularly communicate how many hours you are spending on their projects. Also, for each request they make, tell them roughly how many hours it will take. Nobody likes to be surprised by a giant bill.

WHEN TO USE IT:

Hourly structures are best used in maintenance situations. Perhaps you have finished a website project and the client would like you to make occasional site updates. Or you did a stationery package and the client would like you to create business cards for a new employee.

sources: Burn Your Portfolio by Michael Janda

PRICING STRATEGIES: RETAINER

Retainers are also based on hours spent on a project. Typically you give clients a discounted rate for guaranteeing you hours (usually by month). For example, if your standard rate is $100 per hour and you are pitching your clients a retainer structure, you could discount the rate based on the number of hours they retain. (If the clients retains 20-to-40 hours per month, they pay $90 per hour; 41-to-60 hours per month, they pay $80 per hour; 61-to-80 hours per month, they pay $70 per hour, and so on.) Retainers are purchasing a bucket of hours to be used for client requests. Those hours are usually spread across whatever team members are necessary to complete the request.

DESIGNER

Pros

◈ You get guaranteed monthly billings. This can give you cash flow and the confidence to allow you to hire new employees or expand your business in other ways against the retainer.

Cons

◈ By reducing your rate based on hours retained, you are also reducing your profit margin.

◈ As with the previously mentioned hourly pricing structure, value pricing does not apply.

CLIENT

Pros

◈ By paying a reduced rate for guaranteed hours, clients get more work for less money.

Cons

◈ In this pricing structure, clients have a responsibility to fill the retained hours or they lose them. If they retain 40 hours per month and use only 38 hours, they still pay for the 40 hours.

⚠ ISSUES TO WATCH OUT FOR:

Since clients are retaining hours, you must be extremely attentive to their needs until the hours are used up. Keeping an accurate accounting of the hours for proper billing is important. Oftentimes clients will have a challenge understanding that they are purchasing a block of hours from you and that, whether they use them or not, you have made arrangements in your business to have those hours available for them. If clients use more hours than the agreed-upon retainer, they should pay for the extra hours. We typically charge their retained rate plus 10 percent for all extra hours beyond the retainer. (For example, if clients are retaining 80 hours per month and they use 90 hours, they pay $70 per hour for the first 80 hours and $77 per hour for the extra 10 hours.) The reason for the increased cost attached to extra hours is to accommodate for the unanticipated workload. For example, if you are expecting 80 hours of work and your clients pile on 90 hours, you may have to pay bonuses to accommodate employees staying late, as well as other administrative costs, which may increase your in-house cost for those extra 10 hours.

WHEN TO USE IT:

Retainers work best when clients know that they have an ample amount of projects needing completion over a set amount of time but they are still unclear of the details.

sources: Burn Your Portfolio by Michael Janda

HOW TO CALCULATE A BURN RATE

How can you know how much to charge if you don't know how much your design business costs you per hour? I spent a lot of years pulling prices out of thin air. I had no idea what I should be charging, and to be honest, I was willing to work for whatever someone would pay. As my company began to grow, I quickly learned the importance of understanding total costs. Knowing your costs can help you massage your pricing and land new clients. It can also help you know how much time to allocate to each project.

ANNUAL OVERHEAD COST ÷ ANNUAL PRODUCTION HOURS = HOURLY BURN RATE

You are a freelancer working out of your basement. You decide that you should be earning $60,000 per year for your salary. Your utilities (Internet connection, electricity, cell phone, and so on) cost you roughly $300 per month (or $3,600 per year). Your equipment (computer, stockphoto subscribtion, printer, software upgrades) costs approximately $5,000 per year. Your business expenses (industry and business group annual fees, car mileage, paper, business licenses) cost about $2,000 per year. Don't forget to factor in all vendor expenses (accountant fees, being one) at a typical rate of $1,500 per year.

$60,000 + $3,600 + $5,000 + $2,000 + $1,500 = $72,100 Total Annual Overhead

The average number of work hours in a calendar year

for a nine-to-five employee ranges from 2,080 to 2,096, depending on holidays and specific business practices.

I will use 2,080 hours as our number. Assuming you are self-employed, don't forget that it takes administrative time to run your business. Let's say you spend 10 percent of your time doing nonproduction tasks to keep your business running. That leaves you with 1,872 production hours per year that you can bill for if the project pipeline is full. Now you have your numbers. Run them through the formula to figure out what you must charge per hour to break even.

$72,100 ÷ 1,872 = $38.51

Your hourly burn rate is $38.51. Now you can safely set a rate for your clients and understand where your wiggle room is. But you cannot go below $38.51 per hour without losing money (or paying yourself less than your desired salary of $60,000). You also can make a judgment call on what you want to spend your time doing. I got really crazy at one point and started thinking, "If it takes me three hours to mow my lawn, that will cost me $115.53! I'm better off hiring the neighbor kid to do it for $30...that's $85.53 back in my pocket!"

Now that you have a burn rate, the profitability calculation is easy. Simply tack on a profitability percentage to the hourly burn rate and you will have an hourly rate to charge your clients. If your burn rate is $38.51 and you feel a 20 percent profit margin is fair, then you should charge your customer $46.21 per hour.

Calculating a Burn Rate does not take into consideration the value of a project.
This is important for two reasons, first of all the value might be higher than your official hourly rate, or it may be lower.
Bringing value into the picture of pricing is very important. Which brings us into Cost, Value & Budget.

sources: Burn Your Portfolio by Michael Janda

COST, VALUE & BUDGET

1) COST

The first component that must be considered when estimating your work is cost. This can be done by either determining a fair hourly rate and adding up the number of hours you expect the project to take or by figuring out your exact hourly cost (divide your annual overhead by your production hours available in the year) and then adding a profit margin percentage on top.

2) VALUE

The second element for consideration is the fair market value of the project. Just because you can nail a logo design in one hour doesn't mean you should only charge the client $60. There is a value to the logo that far outweighs $60. Every designer should have The Graphic Artists Guild Handbook: Pricing & Ethical Guidelines. A new issue of the book comes out every few years, and it contains categorized pricing for each type of graphic-design service based on survey averages from design professionals nationwide. This is a great place to get an idea of what fair market value is for design work. Please keep in mind when reviewing the survey averages that the expertise of the design professionals and size of their companies is not reflected in the pricing. If the survey says a brochure for a medium-size business should cost $8,000 and you are a wet-behind-the-ears college graduate, don't expect to be able to green light a brochure at that price. The objective is to gain a sense of what other people, similar to you, charge for the same types of projects you are trying to land.

3) BUDGET

Finally you must have a sense of what the client's budget is for the project. If you wrongly assume the budget is high, then you may send an estimate that prices you out of getting the project when you would have been happy charging less and landing the work. If you wrongly assume the budget is low, then you may undercharge for the work and not be able to turn a profit on the project. Now that you have these three components for consideration, it is time for the balancing act. Let's throw a few darts at the board.

A client wants you to complete Project X: You expect the project will take you 10 hours at your hourly rate of $60 = $600 and that the project has a fair market value of $2,000 based on industry averages. The client has a budget of $1,000 so a simple approach would be to average these three elements and send your client the estimate ($600 + $2,000 + $1,000 = $3,600 ÷ 3 = $1,200). Unfortunately it is not always as simple as just averaging out the numbers based on the variables. There are times when you must skew toward one of the three components.

A client wants you to complete Project Y: You expect the project will take you 100 hours at your hourly rate of $60 = $6,000 and determine the project has a fair market value of $15,000 based on industry averages. The client has a budget of $7,000. If you want to land the work, you must steer your estimate toward the client's budget. My recommendation would be to balance it somewhere in between your hourly cost and the client's budget, $6,750 or so. You are still way below fair market value but still in a zone where you can turn a profit on the project.

A client wants you to complete Project Z: You expect the project will take you 200 hours at your hourly rate of $60 = $12,000 and determine that the project has a fair market value of $18,000 based on industry averages. The client has a budget of $25,000. In this case you could estimate the project in the $18,000 range. Depending on your relationship comfort level, you could then inform the client that your market research indicated that this type of project is costing less than what was budgeted and that you didn't feel it would be fair to charge the full-budgeted amount. This type of move usually goes over very well and could be a great way to start off a project.

In the end, there certainly seems to be a dartboard involved in fixed-bid pricing. Use your best judgment on which component you should skew your price toward. The better you understand the project, your client, and that client's expectations, the easier the pricing will be.

Breaking the Time Barrier by Mike McDerment

this takes value to an extreme, it doesn't always work, but it's worth the read

BREAKING THE TIME BARRIER

Friday Steve stepped into Karen's cafe, a cozy spot with leather chairs and shelves lined with old books. He looked around, taking in the aroma of fresh coffee, then made his way to a back table, where Karen was waiting for him.

After Karen greeted him warmly he settled into his chair, thanking her for meeting with him.

"I'm happy to help," she said before a server came and took their order. Then Karen invited Steve to sketch out his solopreneur journey, which he did over the clatter of coffee cups that surrounded them.

When Steve was done she gave him a one-word verdict: "Pricing."

"Pricing?" he asked.

She nodded as their coffees arrived. "Well... pricing and positioning. From what you've told me, it sounds like the way you think about pricing is holding you back."

"In what way?"

"If someone wanted to know what exactly you sell to your clients, what would you tell them?"

"My services. Web design."

"How do you charge for your services?"

"I charge them a fee based on my hourly rate."

"Then aren't you really selling hours?" Karen asked. "But I use those hours to design websites."

"Do those websites have any positive impact on your clients?"

"Sure," Steve said.

"Do you think it would make more sense to charge a fixed fee that represents the value of the impact your websites have on your clients?"

"Well, I do mostly charge fixed fees—"

"But those fees are based on a multiple of your hours, right?"

"Right," he said.

"I'm talking about fixed fees based on value, not time." "I guess I'm not sure what you mean by value."

"The value of what I do," Karen said, "is based on the impact I can have on my client's business. Impact is how they value my services. So I look at pricing from their point of view. They don't hire me to design a website for the sake of designing a website. They hire me to design a website that's going to help them grow their business. I find when I look at it like that— from their perspective—it's clear I'm not selling time. Instead, I'm selling a solution that is going to make an impact for my client and achieve some business objective."

"So, how do you set your prices then?"

"The value of what I do is based on the impact I can have on my client's business."

"Let me give you an example. A couple of months ago I sat down with a client to talk about their website. I asked them to tell me why they thought they needed a website. When we drilled down into their reasons, they said they believed a website could generate an additional $100,000 of profit annually for their business. So I asked them to make an investment of $20,000 in the website. Based on your hourly pricing model, you'd probably charge in the area of $2,000 to $2,500."

"Did they agree to your price?"

"Yes. Wouldn't you invest $20,000 to generate $100,000?"

Steve agreed and he was excited about what Karen was telling him, but lots of questions were flooding his brain. "I get your math," he said, "but doesn't it come down to time in the end anyway? I mean, you spend a certain amount of time on the project. You could theoretically work out your hourly rate and so could your client. You're probably effectively charging $400 an hour, or something like that. What if your client thinks that's too high?"

"Your math may be right, but I'm not a collection of hours," Karen said. "I'm the accumulation of all my skills and talents. I'm wisdom and creativity. I've stopped seeing myself as a punch card. My clients don't see me that way either. Yes, sometimes, I've had to change my client's mindset. But it starts with me, first, just as it starts with you. You have to forget selling time. The best thing you could do for yourself is to get the concept of time out of your head."

"Don't I need an hourly rate for some stuff? Everyone I know has one."

"You know me now, and I don't have an hourly rate."

"So I should never charge by the hour?"

"I'm the accumulation of all my skills and talents. I'm wisdom and creativity."

READ the ebook:
http://www.freshbooks.com/breaking-the-time-barrier

Why You Shouldn't Charge by the Hour

by: Matthew Griffin
Feb 25th, 2008
in Business & Process

⊕ IT'S TIME CONSUMING

Constantly starting and stopping timers is an annoying and time-consuming practice—it's completely counter-productive. Also, heaven forbid you forget to start the timer or forget about the time altogether. Then you'll end up with a compounded time-consuming mess. Flat-rate billing circumvents this problem completely.

⊕ IT MAKES CLIENTS NERVOUS

You would be surprised how much more comfortable your clients will be if they know exactly how much they are going to spend. Open-ended hourly billing, even accompanied by a ballpark figure, makes buyers nervous. Flat-rate billing makes them feel secure even if they know they'll most likely end up spending more.

⊕ IT ENCOURAGES LOWER PRODUCTIVITY

When you're getting paid by the hour, there's no incentive to work faster or smarter. In fact, the slower you work, the more you get paid. Flat-rate billing encourages you to work efficiently.

⊕ IT FRUSTRATES THE CLIENT

One common misconception about hourly billing is that it puts an end to feature creep. In reality, all it does is frustrate the client. I their mind, every time they ask for something that should have been included in your original time estimate, they're being hit with unfair additional charges. Start with a flat rate with plenty of padding for feature creep, and this will rarely happen.

⊕ IT SEVERELY CRIPPLES BILLING POTENTIAL

Imagine giving an $3,000 estimate for a very basic website. Let's say you've been designing websites for awhile and you're getting pretty fast—you know it will take you about ten full hours of work to get the project finished. Billing by the hour, puts your rate at $300 per hour. It sounds outrageous when you put it in those terms. They have no idea how much work and effort it's taken to hone your skills to their current level. That same site may have taken you fifty hours when you first started designing websites. Flat-rate billing allows you to charge what your services are really worth.

⊕ IT ENCOURAGES CLIENTS TO ABUSE YOU

When you charge by the hour clients tend to argue and grumble about every little charge because they can see every little charge on the invoice. When clients feel that you're cheating them by not working fast enough, they can get really grumpy. Flat-rate billing keeps everybody happy.

I've had great success with flat-rate billing and will continue to stand by it. It's not just a little better than hourly billing; it's night and day. If you manage flat-rate billing correctly, you'll never look back. That's not to say it will solve every billing problem you've ever had, but it sure will solve a lot of them.

source: www.davidairey.com

HOW DESIGNERS CHARGE THEIR CLIENTS

I asked a few designers these questions:
1. How do you charge clients?
2. How do you accept payment?
3. Why do you recommend working this way?

ANTONIO CARUSONE, OF AISLEONE

1. How do you charge clients?
I charge mostly by an hourly rate. I try to estimate how many hours I will work on the project that way I can ask for a percentage of the charge upfront before I begin work.

2. How do you accept payment?
Pretty much always a cheque.

3. Why do you recommend working this way?
Charging hourly seems to yield a more realistic payment over say a flat rate, unless of course you work less than the total flat rate, which almost never happens. Also it's a good idea to ask for a percentage of the payment up front just in case the client decides to bail on you. And cheques are easy to deal with and are more professional than asking for cash.

CHRIS SPOONER, OF SPOON GRAPHICS

1. How do you charge clients?
Once a range of information has been gathered about the project I estimate the costings based on the average number of hours, this is multiplied by my personal hourly rate and supplied as an overall cost. This estimate is then sent over to the client for approval, when the client is happy to start work on the project an initial 50% deposit is collected. The project gets underway and design material is produced. Upon completion the final invoice for the remaining 50% is created, or total remaining balance if additional changes or features have been introduced during the project.

2. How do you accept payment?
I accept Bank Transfers, PayPal, and cheques, with PayPal being the most common form of payment, particularly with overseas clients. The integrated payment system with FreshBooks invoicing app. also allows online invoice payments via PayPal, which can be handy in streamlining the process, immediately marking the invoice as paid.

3. Why do you recommend working this way?
Working on a 50% deposit is definitely recommended, from a designer's point of view it acts as both protection and a deterrent against unscrupulous clients who may be tempted to skip payment. I have yet to find a client who has any issue with an up front payment, with most being more than happy and even expecting to pay up front. From the client's point of view this also helps show how the designer values their service and work.
In terms of payment solutions, bank transfers are my favourite method of payment given the speed and ease, unfortunately this becomes a little tricky when overseas work is involved. This is where PayPal steps in, although the fees do tend to be a little depressing! But I suppose these are relative when considering the benefits.

HOW DESIGNERS CHARGE THEIR CLIENTS

source: www.davidairey.com

I asked a few designers these questions:
1. How do you charge clients?
2. How do you accept payment?
3. Why do you recommend working this way?

BRIAN YERKES, OF BRIAN JOSEPH STUDIOS

1. How do you charge clients?

I provide a full project estimate and present it to the client along with a proposal. I then charge the client 50% of the project total up front to be paid before the project commences. The final 50% is required once the project is completed.

My estimates are based on two factors:

My hourly rate
Competitor's rates
Knowledge is power, and knowing what your competitors are charging is vital to ensure that you are able to place your company at the price point you want to be at, whether it is at the high end or the low end.

For smaller pieces of work, like a few updates to a website page and if it is less than $1,000, I require 100% up front.been introduced during the project.

2. How do you accept payment?

We accept cheques and credit cards. I am slightly torn on whether or not to continue excepting credit cards as you obviously lose that 3% of each transaction. It is a good thing for your clients however, especially those with tight budgets. It allows them to pay for your services and put it on credit rather than having to have the money in available cash at that time.

For larger projects, we require that the client pays the initial 50% by cheque. This seems to ensure that the client at least has a decent amount of money at their disposal, and it gives us more of a secure feeling that we will receive the final 50% when the project has been completed.

One negative aspect of receiving cheques is that you have to wait to receive it in the post. If you have a client in another country, this process can take a few days. This is where bank transfers, and PayPal can help a lot.

3. Why do you recommend working this way?

I would recommend requiring 50% up front because it asks the client to put commitment into the project. At a certain point during the project, you are working over what the initial 50% will cover, so for the remainder of the project, you are then showing your commitment to the client, as you work towards the final payment. This keeps the playing field level for both of you and provides a nice basis for a working relationship.

HOW DESIGNERS CHARGE THEIR CLIENTS

I asked a few designers these questions:
1. How do you charge clients?
2. How do you accept payment?
3. Why do you recommend working this way?

YAEL MILLER, OF THE DIELINE

1. How do you charge clients?
On smaller-mid sized projects I require a 50% deposit and the balance prior to release of production-ready files. On larger (longer-term) projects with several stages of deliverables, I require the same 50% deposit prior to starting any work, but break up the fee schedule based on deliverables. A retainer is usually applied to the end of the project, too.

2. How do you accept payment?
I accept wire (bank) transfer for overseas clients, paypal when a client prefers this or is in a rush, and most often for US based clients — a cheque by mail. I usually charge a small fee to cover the wire transfer and paypal payment methods.

3. Why do you recommend working this way?
This works for me. It spreads the risk yet gives the client (who may be a first time client in many cases) the option of not paying everything at once to an unknown designer/studio. It's a pretty fair process. The only added advice is that even if a client has 'proven' themselves to be trustworthy by having paid your deposit and even subsequent payments, you must not continue to provide work into future phases of a project before getting payments as per the signed agreement / fee schedule. I have learned this the hard way. Trust me — it's worth swallowing your pride and overcoming any fear of confrontation and not moving forward on a project until you get payment as per your mutual agreed-upon contract. Many unexpected things can come up – even personal emergencies or as we now know — catastrophic economic upheavals — that can upend even a trustworthy and fair client's willingness or ability to pay you.

STEVEN SNELL, OF VANDELAY DESIGN

1. How do you charge clients?
I usually charge a flat rate based on the project, although I do have a few ongoing clients that usually get billed by the hour. Issues like charging in advance vary somewhat. If I'm working with an ongoing client then I just charge after the work is done, but with a new client I'll typically charge part up front, but the percentage isn't always consistent. This is something I should probably do a little better is to develop more consistency.

2. How do you accept payment?
I either get paid by PayPal or by cheque. Clients who are friends, family or referrals usually prefer to pay by cheque, but people that find me online and live in various parts of the US or the world typically pay with PayPal. I prefer PayPal.

3. Why do you recommend working this way?
I recommend having some flexibility with accepting payment because clients have different preferences. I also recommend charging upfront, although as I mentioned I need more consistency in the percentage. When I first started freelancing I got into some difficult situations that could have been avoiding by charging up front. I had one situation where I didn't get paid for several hours of work and a few other situations where it would have been helpful to get more up front to get more commitment and urgency from clients.

BEWARE OF LINE-ITEM PRICING

PRICING STRATEGIES

sources: Burn Your Portfolio by Michael Janda

⚠ ISSUES TO WATCH OUT FOR:

Warning: Beware of estimating cost this way! I've been burned more times than I'd like to admit by this pricing strategy. The client will look at this breakdown and decide that they can live without the letterhead and envelopes and then ask to pull those elements from the project, leaving me with $1,200 to do a job that is probably still worth closer to the $2000 mark than the $1200 I will now be making. The realities of this project is that most of the design work is done in the Logo Design phase. You put the brainpower into this part, and as you are designing the logos, you are making mental considerations for how the designs will convert into the other stationery elements. Also after you design the business cards, the letterhead and envelope will be a piece of cake. The truth of the matter is that the cost breakdown for this project would be something closer to Option B.

Most clients will be drawn to fixed-bid pricing. They want to know exactly what the project is going to cost, and they expect you to stay on budget. From the designer's side, fixed-bid pricing isn't altogether bad, since you will know exactly how much budget you will have to execute the project.

When I first started freelancing, I worked exclusively via fixed-bid pricing scales. A client would send me the specs for a project, and I would attach pricing to the project and gain the client's approval for that amount. First I would calculate how long the whole job would take, and then I would break it into itemized pricing. For example, if a client wants a logo design along with a stationery package, I would estimate that I would need about two days of production to complete the whole project. So if I attach a cost of $2,000 to the project to help the client get an idea of where the costs lie, I would spread out the $2,000 across all the elements of the project.

OPTION A:
Logo design–$800
Business card design–$400
Letterhead design–$400
Envelope design–$400
TOTAL: $2000

OPTION B:
Logo design–$1600
Business card design–$200
Letterhead design–$100
Envelope design–$100
TOTAL: $2000

OPTION C:
Logo design,
Business card design, Letterhead design, Envelope design
TOTAL: $2000

OPTION D:
Project management–$300
Design–$1,000
Production–$700
TOTAL: $2000

Each of these items would be explained in the proposal so the client knew exactly what was included for each element. I felt cool. This line-item pricing looked legit and organized. Look at me! I'm a graphic designer sending out fancy bids.

However, with this line-item pricing the client will look at it and possibly balk at the $1600 logo price. Most small businesses would rather have their cousin's friend's brother design their logo on trade for a new pair of sneakers than pay $1600 for their logo design. So you shouldn't send this type of line-item pricing either.

In the end sending the client one lump-sum price like Option C is better than the previous options, but this isn't a great solution either since breaking out the costs helps the client swallow a big quote easier (kind of like when you go to get your car fixed at an auto repair shop).

So what is a designer to do? You will need to break out pricing more in line with the realities of the project. Detail exactly what the client is going to get (deliverables) and then break down the pricing in this fashion.

Project Management includes deliveries, phone calls, and administrative elements required to execute on the project. Design covers the creative tasks, and Production covers creation of press-ready files. With this strategy, the pricing is itemized so that the client can understand how you arrived at the total price. But none of the itemized elements can be removed from the project (as they could in Option A) without requiring you to send a revised estimate to the client.

THE SOLUTION

There will be times when a client will force you to break down a project as in Option A; they want to know exactly what each item will cost. If you must do so to win the job, then you must. Be careful when breaking down the price of any specific item (such as Design), and ask yourself these critical questions when you look at your numbers: If the client pulls any one item out of this cost breakdown, will I still be happy with the total price of the job? If an item is pulled, will I still be able to execute on the other elements at the individual prices as they are quoted? If you answer no to either question, then rework the numbers until you are satisfied. When a client forces you into itemizing a project, then you have to assume that pulling elements out is being considered. Brace yourself and tread lightly.

PROPOSAL DOCUMENT STRUCTURES

We have examined all of the parts that can be included in a design proposal. There is a time and place for inclusion of each content part. In this section we'll analyze several types of proposal document structures and provide some insight on when to use each of them.

1 MINI-PROPOSALS

It is not always appropriate to send a big, full-blown proposal either. A Mini-Proposal is a smaller scale proposal document used in certain situations. It includes the following proposal content parts:
- Cover Page
- Project Summary
- Pricing

A Mini-Proposal is just the thing to help in two scenarios:
1. If you are questioning whether the potential client has adequate budget to pay for the project requested, you should send a Mini-Proposal prior to creation of a larger-scale proposal. If you use a Mini-Proposal in this manner, I recommend sending it to the potential client with a message like this, "Prior to embarking on the task of creating a full-blown proposal, I just wanted to make sure we were on the same page by sending you a Mini- Proposal. This proposal includes a Project Summary and an initial Pricing estimation. If both of these elements seem in line with your expectations, please let me know and we'll proceed in creating a larger proposal that will define in detail the Statement of Work, Deliverables, Project Scope, and Timeline aspects of the project." The Mini-Proposal usually does a good job of flushing out the validity of a questionable client.
2. We have several long-term clients who green-light work without requiring a proposal from our agency. While they may not require a formal proposal, we have learned that it is best to always create some type of proposal. We need a proposal to track the project in our accounting system and to send the client some documentation on what we are creating for the agreed-upon price. In these situations, we usually email the client a PDF Mini-Proposal with a message like the following, "I know we have already started the project and we're on the same page for scope and pricing. However, our systems require a formal proposal so we can track the project properly in our accounting system. Attached is a Mini-Proposal to make sure our accountant stays happy. Please let me know if you have any questions."
3. It's for a small project.

2 SMALL-MEDIUM PROPOSALS

Most proposals seem to fall into this category. Small- Medium Proposals include all of the essential items used to properly scope the project as well as the content parts necessary to protect the interests of both the agency and the client. These content parts include the following:
- Cover Page
- Project Summary
- Statement of Work
- Deliverables
- Project Scope Checklist
- Feedback Rounds
- Pricing
- Timeline
- Terms & Conditions
- Proposal Acceptance

This proposal document structure is often used with clients you've worked with in the past. It is formal and clearly establishes a plan for the project. As with any proposal, other content parts can be added to this base structure as necessary to help your chances of landing the project. You may consider adding About Us, Design Strategy, Technical Strategy, or Case Studies to further define your qualifications for the project.

3 LARGE PROPOSALS

Big time projects for big time clients require everything and the kitchen sink. If you really want to show off the range of your expertise and your full scope of qualifications for a project, you should include all of the proposal content parts in your document. Your proposal should be bound and you should review it in a formal meeting with your client.
- Cover Page
- Introduction Letter
- Table of Contents
- Project Summary
- Statement of Work
- Deliverables
- Project Scope Checklist
- Feedback Rounds
- Pricing
- Timeline
- Keys to Project Success
- Design Strategy
- Technical Strategy
- About Us
- Team Bios
- Testimonials
- Our Process
- Case Studies
- Terms & Conditions
- The Code of Fair Practice
- Proposal Acceptance

SAMPLE ONE PAGE QUOTATION
For small Projects
check out: webdesignquote.beewits.com

QUOTATION

Date

Designers Name
Designers Address

CLIENT CONTACT NAME

Project Description

Project Description	QTY	Price Per QTY	Total
		$100	$100
Description	1	$100	$100
Project Management	1	$100	$100
Design time	1	$100	$100
Content / copy	1	$100	$100
Development	1		
Template			$100
Other Expenses		Sub Total	$600
Other		Tax	3%
		Total Estimated	$618

Quote issued by | 123 Your Address Your City, State, Country.
Trading Name: Trading Name
Email: youremail@server.com | **Tel:** 123456789 | **Website**

Stock photos are included in the price. If you decide you would like a specific stock photo, not from our library, you will be charged separately. This quote does not include custom photography, digital rendering of photos or illustration. Comps will be sent to you within 20 business days for when all the information is recieved. If you should need a rush on this, there will be an additional fee of 20% of the final cost. We need all the information and photos for the project before we begin. This project is expected to be completed within 30 days time. If this project exceeds 30 days the remainder balance will be due and the project can be restarted based on the designers availability, at the additional rate of $XX.00 an hour. Please read the "Code of Fair Practice" (https://www.graphicartistsguild.org/tools_resources/the-code-of-fair-practice-for-the-graphic-communications-industry1) by sending the deposit you are agreeing to their terms. Upon full payment, the client obtains ownership of the final high resolution design file, and may use and distribute as they see fit. We reserve the right to use any elements of the design in future work. Above information is not an invoice and only an estimate of services described above. This estimate is non-contractual. If you have any questions concerning this invoice, please get back to us using the contact details above. Thank you for your business!

sources: Burn Your Portfolio by Michael Janda

PROJECT SCOPE CHECKLIST

Scope Creep is alive and well in the creative services industry. If you don't adequately define the project in your proposal, some clients will try to take advantage of you and increase the scope of the project. Statement of Work and Deliverables sections should clearly describe the services you are going to provide and the deliverables clients are going to receive. But what about the things you are NOT going to do? The Project Scope Checklist serves two purposes and is the final step to clarifying your project in detail.

First, it will provide you and your potential clients with a quick overview of what is (and what is not) included in the scope of the project. Second, the Project Scope Checklist provides your clients with insight into other services you offer that they may not have known about.

BRANDING

DELIVERABLE / SERVICE	YES	NO
Branding Exercise		X
Concept Sketches		X
Mood Boards		X
Color Stories		X
Logo Design		X
Logo Variations / Logo Family		X
Icon Design		X
Mini Style Guide		X
Full Style Guide		X

PRINT

DELIVERABLE / SERVICE	YES	NO
Brochure Design		X
Business Card Design		X
Letterhead Design		X
Envelope Design		X
One Sheet Design		X
Annual Report Design		X
Poster Design		X
Coordination of Printing		X
Press Checks		X
Printing Costs		X

GENERAL

DELIVERABLE / SERVICE	YES	NO
Copywriting		X
Custom Photography / Photo Shoots		X
Stock Photo Purchases		X
Custom Illustration		X
Focus Group Management		X
Font Purchases		X
Market Analysis & Strategy		X
Client Requested Travel		X
Client Requested After-hours Staffing		X
Marketing Campaign Management		X
Media Buying		X

WEB/DIGITAL

DELIVERABLE / SERVICE	YES	NO
Content Inventory		X
Wireframe Pages		X
Site Map		X
Website Design		X
Front-End Development		X
Back-End Development		X
Responsive Design		X
Responsive Development		X
Custom Animation		X
Functional Prototypes		X
GUI (Graphical User Interface) Templates		X
GUI Style Guide		X
HTML5 & JavaScript Programming		X
Flash Programming		X
PHP Programming		X
ASP Programming		X
.NET Programming		X
Java Programming		X
PYTHON Programming		X
CMS Integration		X

DELIVERABLES

The Deliverables section of your proposal will answer the client's question, "What am I going to get?" This section and the Pricing section are often where the potential client will focus the most attention. That client wants to make sure that at the end of the day the expected product will be delivered at the promised price.

Your final Deliverables list should be detailed and organized.

To create your Deliverables list you should examine each section of your Statement of Work and ask yourself the question, "What are the tangible items I am going to deliver to the client during this phase of the project?"

EXAMPLE OF BROCHURE DELIVERABLES

- Initial design comps (a minimum of three) delivered in JPEG format
- Revised design comps as requested and in accordance with the Feedback Rounds guidelines in this proposal
- Final design comp (One design for final approval prior to creation of press-ready files)
- Final approved design delivered to client in press-ready format including printer's marks and high-resolution images

Take time to describe in detail what you will be providing the client during each phase of the project. Provide specific numbers wherever possible. However, keep in mind that many clients will be sticklers for the numbers. If you promise five comps but land on a design that everyone loves after the third comp, there are clients who will try to squeeze you for a discount. With this in mind, I recommend attaching minimum and maximum to your numeric descriptions. By saying "a minimum of three comps," you are free to explore additional creative solutions for the project without contractual obligation in the proposal. Additional comps will then be seen as added value for

the client and help you exceed expectations. However, if you list "three-to-five comps," as the Deliverable and only deliver three, some clients may feel disappointed having expected the larger number.

source: www.davidairey.com

STATEMENT OF WORK

As you can see from the broken-down descriptions, your potential client will have a much clearer picture of the services you intend to provide for them. The Statement of Work serves to answer the client's question, "What is the vendor going to do?"

The Statement of Work is the proposal's most critical section for both the vendor and the client. A detailed Statement of Work will serve to protect the vendor from scope creep and he-said, she-said moments that tend to occur when working with some clients. For the client the Statement of Work is an assurance that you fully understand the project and will provide the services needed. A loosely written Statement of Work will get you into trouble. You never want to be in a situation where you think you are building a 15-page website only to find that your client is expecting a 50-page website. Spare no detail when writing the Statement of Work.

1 BREAK DOWN EACH DELIVERABLE INTO SERVICES

It Break down the deliverables into services. For example, if you are going to build a website, you should break down the deliverable Website as Website UX, Website Design, and Website Programming. If you are going to create a print brochure for a client, you could break down Brochure into smaller details like Copywriting, Design/Layout, Prepress, and Press Coordination. There is no hard-and-fast rule as to how to subdivide each service you will be providing. Use vernacular familiar to you and your client.

2 DESCRIBE EACH SERVICE IN DETAIL

Now that you have a breakdown of each service you will be providing, describe each in detail. Try to be specific wherever possible and appropriate. The tendency for most designers is to be too general when specifics are required. While writing the description of each service you should be asking yourself questions like these:
- What exactly are we going to be doing for this client?
- Will the client know what I am talking about or do I need to explain? (For example, some clients may know what UI/ UX or a press check is while others may have no clue what you are talking about.)
- What are the specific details I can include here? Print dimensions and page quantity? Website page quantity? Logo version quantity?
- What will the client be expecting during each phase of
- the project?
- What concerns will the client have about this item? Have I adequately addressed those concerns in my description?

DETAILS OF BROCHURE DELIVERABLE EXAMPLE

Most designers have a tendency to want to describe only the deliverable. Here is an example statement for the deliverable Brochure: "Awesome Agency will create a marketing brochure for the company. The brochure will be designed as a trifold brochure, 8.5 by 11 inches and will contain copy and images to promote the company."

The problem with this statement is that your client is paying for the services you are providing in addition to the deliverable. To arrive at the final Brochure deliverable, you must utilize your expertise and execute on a myriad of tasks. Each of those tasks should be clearly explained in your proposal. In addition to protecting you against future changes in scope, documenting what you are going to do for the client will help create a better appreciation of your expertise and a higher level of confidence in your ability to execute on the requested work. Here is an example of how the Brochure project could be detailed in your Statement of Work:
- Brochure Design/Layout: Awesome Agency will take the approved copy and design a brochure that will meet the client's marketing needs. The brochure design will follow existing branding guidelines established by the client's other marketing materials. It is anticipated that the brochure will be 8.5 by 11 inches folded into three panels. The brochure design will also be in color on front and back.
- Brochure Prepress: Following approval of the final brochure design, Awesome Agency will prepare the files for press.
- All images will be integrated at press resolution (300 dpi). The final document will be an Adobe InDesign file. Proper printer's marks will be added to the final file and all colors and fonts will be verified as press ready.

Congratulations!
Today is your day.
You're off to Great Places!
You're off and away!

You have brains in your head.
You have feet in your shoes.
You can steer yourself
any direction you choose.
You're on your own. And you know
what you know.
And YOU are the guy who'll decide
where to go.

You'll look up and down streets. Look
'em over with care.
About some you will say, "I don't
choose to go there."
With your head full of brains and your
shoes full of feet,
you're too smart to go down any not-
so-good street.

And you may not find any
you'll want to go down.
In that case, of course,
you'll head straight out of town.

It's opener there
in the wide open air.

Out there things can happen
and frequently do
to people as brainy
and footsy as you.

And then things start to happen,
don't worry. Don't stew.
Just go right along.
You'll start happening too.

OH!
THE PLACES YOU'LL GO!

—Dr. Seuss

I want to thank you for giving me the oppurtunity to join you on your journey to become a graphic designer. It's amazing to watch your work develop and grow.
I would love to see where you are going to take this.
Please keep in touch!
Wishing you all the best!

Chaya Murik

Printed in Dunstable, United Kingdom